TAKING
CONTROL
of your
FINANCIAL
LIFE

TAKING CONTROL

of your

FINANCIAL LIFE

HOW TO HAVE **FINANCIAL FREEDOM** AND **PEACE OF MIND**

Julian Rubinstein

BMD

PUBLISHING

TAKING CONTROL OF YOUR FINANCIAL LIFE
How to Have Financial Freedom and Peace of Mind

COPYRIGHT © 2024 JULIAN RUBINSTEIN

ISBN # 979-8877884199

BMD Publishing
BMDPublishing@MarketDominationLLC.com
www.MarketDominationLLC.com

BMD Publishing CEO: Seth Greene
Editorial Management: Bruce Corris
Technical Editor, Layout & Cover Design: Kristin Williams

Printed in the United States of America.

ACKNOWLEDGMENTS

This has been an exciting and special project for me. It combines my love for my craft with my passion for helping people and potentially changing their lives in a meaningful way.

I want to thank all the talented, successful professionals who participated and agreed to be interviewed for this project, and who shared their vast knowledge and experiences. They all are friendly and easy to do business with, so please feel free to reach out to these professionals when you need their individual expertise.

I dedicate this book to my two terrific daughters, Alexandra & Brooke and my amazing wife, Rebecca. They give meaning to my life and provide the work-life balance I would not have without them. I love all of you very much!

Finally, I would like to thank all of you who took the time to read this book. I hope you find the information useful and worth sharing with others.

CONTENTS

PART 4   BUSINESS FINANCES

INTRODUCTION

Y ou might be asking, "Why do I need to read a book about financial planning?" Maybe talking about money and the future makes you uncomfortable or you're afraid of what an expert might tell you.

The fact of the matter is everyone should be asking the simple and complex questions about their financial future.

Even with everything I have learned about financial success and planning, I am always looking for new ways to help my clients feel confident in achieving financial freedom. That's why I interviewed experts on retirement, asset planning, current market conditions, and investing. Each chapter will provide you expert information on ways to take control of your financial life.

Money can be a tricky subject to broach and many people are unsure about retirement. People who are saving for retirement need growth because they need to build up enough equity to retire. Those that are retired need income to live on. I help my clients navigate these uncertain waters.

People don't plan for their financial future because they are afraid of what it might look like. They're scared of what they might hear, so instead, they put off planning until it's almost too late. Others think they have more money than they do because they don't know certain tax laws or don't know how much they spend. Financial planning is vital for everyone.

I've been in this field for over two decades advising individuals on the right way to invest. I have started and sold businesses, and worked in mergers and acquisitions, and private equity.

I wrote this book to help you understand the current financial markets. My goal is to simplify and address the questions you need answers to so you can begin on the correct path to financial freedom. I want to share my expertise and give you the assurance you need to make important financial decisions in your life. Regardless of your age, financial position, or net worth, this book will help you make informed decisions when it comes to managing your finances.

MEET JULIAN RUBINSTEIN

B efore you hear from the experts and other professionals who can help you navigate the current market and make passive income, let me share a little about myself.

Back in the late 70's, the New York Times was selling the paper at a 50% discount to the students at every university through their College & School program run by a student on campus. When I was a freshman at Syracuse University, that position became available, and I was fortunate to be awarded that franchise. I then reached out to many large corporations such as airlines, moving companies, etc., with great success. By my junior year, the Syracuse administration decided that if a company wanted a presence at the university, they had to hire my services exclusively. By my senior year, I had grown the NY Times into the largest one in the United States. An interview with the college newspaper depicting my business at the university was picked up by the Associated Press. The article was published nationwide & in Canada, which set up my career.

After graduating, I became a sought-after individual and despite having many offers, I chose to join a small manufacturing concern in Montreal that made laundry sinks and shower stalls as their first U.S. sales rep. We hit Home

Depot just as they were starting, and we benefited from the wave of big box stores. As the American business began to grow, the Montreal factory could not meet the demand. I was given 20% equity in the U.S. corporation with an option to purchase an additional 30% equity over five years, based on profit goals along with the task of opening a U.S. manufacturing facility. I hit those goals in two years and became a 50% owner. Shortly thereafter, the Canadian ownership tried to purchase my shares in a hostile takeover. Fortunately, I ended up buying them out. In the ensuing five years, due to a major product packaging change I developed for our shower stalls, I became the largest manufacturer of laundry sinks & corner glass shower stalls in the country. In 1994, I sold the company to Masco Corporation, a public company best known for their brand Delta Faucet. I spent four years with Masco merging & successfully turning around their biggest losing division.

When my earn-out contract with Masco ended, I joined Sun Capital Partners as the first operational partner. After two years, I decided to leave & set up my own investment firm, American Asset Management.

When I started American Asset Management, I was living off my investment portfolio, so I wanted income without loss of principal. Therefore, I decided to concentrate on developing risk averse portfolios that would produce annual income. While the stock market is a good investment in the long run, if you need income from your investments, it can be unnerving to see your money fluctuate by 50% up and down.

In March of 1999 the S&P 500 hit 1,500. It dropped to 650 in March of 2009 and it took until March of 2013 to recover back to 1,500. 14 years of break-even with two drops of more than 50% during that 14-year period. For young investors that is called a buying opportunity while for retired investors that is called a disaster,

Our portfolios are based on Defined Outcome Solutions investing with pre-defined return & risk profiles. These solutions include features such as principal protection, defined annual income and a target growth rate. We use an option strategy & structured notes to provide income with set downside protection and buffered UIT's to provide downside protection along with upside potential from the stock market. In my approach, I strive to create portfolios with the lowest possible volatility because volatility makes people panic. My goal is to have a portfolio that lets you and me sleep at night regardless of what is going on in the financial world.

We serve two primary groups of clients: those who are retired and those who are saving for a house, college, or retirement.

Those who are retired are seeking regular income to sustain their lifestyles without touching their principal. When you retire, it is very important to understand your monthly/annual income needs, so your portfolio can be designed to provide that income. Once you have achieved your income needs you can invest in growth, albeit with downside protection.

One significant mistake retired people often make is getting trapped in misleading annuities that are sold to them. These annuities promise lifetime income, which sounds appealing at first. People think it's perfect because they'll never run out of income. What they fail to realize, however, is that annuities don't provide income. Instead, they offer guaranteed withdrawals. In essence, it means you're receiving your own money back. It's unfortunate that people get lured in by this guarantee, thinking it's what they need, without realizing they're only earning what the 30-year Treasury pays. Over the past decade, many individuals have earned a meager 2-3% on their investments, after accounting for fees. Essentially, they have not made much progress and are essentially taking their own money back. This situation is regrettable, as it leaves nothing for their heirs, for no good reason.

Another unfortunate aspect, particularly in Florida, is the prevalence of seminars offering a free dinner to entice attendees. These events are often orchestrated to sell an annuity rather than to genuinely help individuals invest their money. The motivation behind these seminars is the substantial commission that comes with selling a product.

For younger clients it is important to understand what goal they are saving for. If it's for a house, you are going to need to take a more conservative approach. For children's college education you can get more aggressive, and for retirement you can be much more aggressive. We tailor a portfolio based on each of those different goals and objectives.

When it comes to investing in the stock market, in my opinion, trying to pick individual stocks is akin to legalized gambling. Professional stock pickers have so much more information about a stock than the individual investor. As an example, a professional investor can buy data on how many trucks were at every Home Depot store on any given day. Rather than attempt to pick individual stocks, we use the best no load mutual funds to grow your money wisely.

Young investors need to realize that stock market declines are buying opportunities and should not panic. Think of a stock market decline as a 25% off sale at a department store. You wouldn't walk into a department store having that sale and tell them to call you when everything's back to full price. I'm not trying to be funny, I'm just trying to point out that if you have a long-term time horizon you should want to buy at low prices not high prices.

When it comes to retirement, the rules have changed dramatically as people are living well into their late 80s or 90s. When Social Security was designed, it was assumed that someone retired at 65 and would likely pass away at 75. That was just a 10-year period. Now, if you retire at 65, your money might have to last for at least 25 years. Before you retire, it is very important to know exactly what your expenses will be to make sure you're going to have enough income to live on for the rest of your life. Do not make the mistake of retiring too early as it is one mistake you cannot undo.

One significant project that has consumed much of my time involves the ambitious goal of launching the country's first mutual fund that exclusively invests in structured notes. This is driven by a simple fact: structured notes typically require a minimum investment of $500,000, making them inaccessible to most individuals. While advisors can combine these notes and distribute them among multiple clients, this approach demands a substantial amount of work and poses various challenges. Thus, there exists a clear need for a mutual fund where one can purchase a diversified portfolio of structured notes with as little as $1,000. I am fully dedicated to the task of bringing this fund to life.

When it comes to my investment style, there is one aspect that sets me apart from other investment advisors: I manage my own money in the same way I manage my clients' funds.

If you were to examine my portfolio alongside my clients' portfolios, you would find them mirroring one another. This approach offers two significant advantages. First, I personally invest in the strategies I recommend to my clients, which ensures that I have a vested interest in their success. Second, and perhaps most important, managing portfolios this way allows me to actively monitor each client's account daily.

Most advisors oversee 50 diverse portfolios. Realistically, they can't review all of them that often. Would they be able to attend to each account on a weekly or monthly basis? In contrast, I can assess the markets and track the performance of my portfolios every single day. This enables me to stay on top of the investments much more effectively. This hands-on approach and constant monitoring have been critical to my success in the industry.

While writing this book, I was lucky to have met a lot of interesting people. I got know them and learn about the jobs they have. It's fascinating to see the diverse range of individuals I've had the chance to connect with. I am eager to continue growing my business as it brings me great satisfaction. In the past, during my time in the manufacturing industry, I didn't feel like I was making a significant impact on others' lives. Specializing in manufacturing shower stalls lacked the sense of helping society in a meaningful way. I couldn't ignore the fact that I wasn't contributing much value to society. This realization drove me to transition into the financial sector, where I now assist people in managing their money and ensuring they lead comfortable lives. I am truly passionate about my current work.

The financial world is always filled with problems and concerns that seem insurmountable. The 1929 stock market crash and the Great Depression, Black Monday in 1987, the great financial crisis of 2008 and COVID of 2020. At the time of writing this book we are faced with a war in Ukraine and Israel. We have overcome these horrific times in the past and will continue to do so. If you have the right portfolio designed to meet your individual goals and objectives, you will be fine.

I hope this book gives you a clear idea of how to begin to plan for retirement and the different aspects involved in retirement planning.

Let's begin.

Part 1

GETTING OUT OF DEBT

CHAPTER 1

THE SHRED METHOD

Adam Carroll

Julian: You have a very interesting background and career, so why don't you give us a little bit about you?

Adam: I graduated from college as a debt statistic, as many people do today, and a good friend of mine encouraged me to read a couple of books, ones you probably have on your bookshelf: *Rich Dad, Poor Dad* and *The Cashflow Quadrant*. I immediately was hooked on personal finance; I started reading every book I could get my hands on. I read *The Wealthy Barber* and *The Richest Man in Babylon* and *Think and Grow Rich* and so on, from the 1930s to today.

It occurred to me that if I had read all these books and I was practicing it, then I could probably teach it, so when I was 28, I started a seminar company and started teaching financial literacy to the public. That was my beginning.

Julian: What are you doing now and how did you evolve to this?

Adam: Over the years, as I was doing engagements, I was learning all sorts of things from the people I was speaking with. It occurred to me that lots of folks were dealing with copious amounts of debt, and they were trying to figure out how to make their lives work while also paying down or paying off debt and/or investing at the same time. I was introduced to this idea known as an Australian mortgage.

There was a bank in Australia years ago that, in addition to giving someone a mortgage, would give them what they call the sweep account. Basically, all of your income would go in the sweep account, and that account would allow you to make lump-sum payments to your mortgage, thereby paying your mortgage off quickly. It was probably not a great business model for the bank, but it was great for the users, for the consumers.

A vast majority of Australians at the time did not have mortgages on their properties because of this Australian mortgage. They started bringing this concept over to the United States, and I was introduced to the concept and then found a piece of software that actually does the calculations for you. It would tell you what to do with your income to make sure it was being used in the most efficient way possible.

I ended up procuring the source code from the owner about three years ago, and we're now building a software company where we're teaching people how to deleverage so they can use the equity in their homes to optimize it elsewhere. In effect, we're clawing back some of the interest we're paying to the banks in the early years of our mortgages. Maybe the goal is to pay it off, maybe not; it depends on a person's situation.

But we then ask them, "Okay, now that you have liquidity, where do you place that liquidity to make sure you're making the best use of it?"

Julian: You're having people take out home-equity loans?

Adam: We'll often use a line of credit. It could be home equity. It could be a personal line or a business line of credit. In some cases, when people say, "I don't want to use a HELOC," we'll set up what we would call a shred account. That could be a portion of emergency savings, but we'll also say, "If you need access to money, let's have a line of credit in place, just in case." But you could use that side account, too. That's typically money that hasn't been touched in some time. It's the age-old wisdom of six to 12 months' worth of living expenses in the bank.

Julian: Keep the HELOC for that, but then at least put that six-to-eight months to work.

Adam: That's exactly right.

Julian: What do you usually recommend they do with that money? What kind of investments do you like?

Adam: I am going to go back just a minute on this.

> I've found that the market or retirement as usual may be in question. Many people currently in their mid-60s and early 70s are living on their investments, but when the market declines 20% or 30%, they'll find themselves a little frantic, asking, "Am I going to outlive my money?"

I like the idea of maxing out 401(k)s and Roth IRAs, but I also think there ought to be some alternative investments out there. That could be real estate. That could be syndications. It could be something that's generating passive income, at the very least, because if you're really mapping out your financial future, it's not about working until you're 65 or 70. It's about having enough passive income to supersede your expenses.

That's really what we're after: alternative investments that will generate cashflow.

Julian: We do the same thing. Most of our clients want income, so we really believe that income is important, because growth sounds great until it stops growing, and then it starts declining.

Adam: Exactly.

> The Shred Method begins to create certainty of what the future looks like.

We'll have clients who'll shred their mortgages to a certain extent. Let's say they start with a $500,000 mortgage, and they shred it down to $250,000 or even $200,000 in some cases. Many of them will do that within three or four years; they'll get it down that fast.

Then, what we suggest to them is, "Now that you've got it down and the majority of your payment's going to principal, would you rather have a lower mortgage payment and just have access to that equity?" In which case, we do a recast of the mortgage, so if they still have 26 or 27 years left on their mortgage, they're at a three or four percent interest rate. If they're at six, we have different strategies for that. But at three or four percent, we could recast the mortgage down to $200,000, and in many cases, they'll be left with a $1,000 mortgage payment.

Our goal then is to create enough passive income to supersede their living expenses. That's our goal for people: to live free within five or six years. All housing expenses are covered, and your work could be somewhat optional, but you're working because you enjoy what you do, not because you have to go to work to cover the huge net that you have every month.

Julian: What would you say is the biggest financial mistake people make?

Adam: There is an assumption that their high income is going to last them forever, and so they lifestyle up according to their income. I think that's probably the biggest mistake.

Second to that—and they may be related—there's no real long-term planning. People will look out maybe a year or three years, but I like to plan 20, 30, even 50 years out. What do you want your grandchildren to experience? We can start creating a plan that isn't necessarily restrictive in terms of your lifestyle. You'll make some different choices, perhaps, but some of the sacrifices you make today can make your life look drastically different in 10 years.

Julian: I think people tend to not want to do financial planning because they're afraid of the answer. They're afraid of how much you're going to tell them they have to save in order to retire at a certain age.

Adam: I totally agree, and that's the power of The Shred Method. When someone says, "How would I ever put away $30,000 extra a year, or $100,000 extra a year?", we say, "Well, right now, you're sending $30,000 a year to your bank, or more, depending on the mortgage size." Some people are sending $60,000 a year in interest to their banks.

What if you were sending half that amount to your bank, and the rest was actually building your net worth and creating more equity in your property that you could then displace into something else? What we're doing is not magic, but it is math, and I think this is something that's not really being taught in society today.

Julian: What's something you share with every client? What's your go-to, one piece of advice that you like to share?

Adam: My real go-to is somewhat based on a TED Talk I gave at the London Business School a few years ago, and it's this: **kids are expensive, but they don't have to be.** The USDA says it will cost upwards of $280,000 to raise a child from zero to 18, not including education costs. Yet some of that can be offset by educating your children financially and really bringing them up where they manage their own money.

Too many parents say, "I love my kids. I don't want them to struggle." In reality, the struggle is what makes us able to survive life's lows, so we want our kids to struggle financially when they're young. My son asked me one day, "Dad, are we rich?" I said, "What makes you ask that?" He said, "Well, some of my buddies were talking. The neighbors bought a new Tesla, and they've also got this other car in their driveway, and so they were talking about them being rich. Are we rich?" I said, "Son, your mom and I are very comfortable. You have nothing."

A lot of parents tell their kids, "Oh, yeah, we're rich," meaning, "My parents are well-off, and therefore I am also well-off." The kids grow up thinking they are well-off and start to spend like they are, and then quickly realize they're actually not, or they're on their parents' financial-economic-outpatient-support plan, which doesn't work.

Julian: I always joke: The one thing kids never leave, though, is your cellphone plan.

Adam: That is true.

Julian: So, do you also do workshops and speaking engagements?

Adam: I do. There was a point in time in my life when I'd do 50 or 60 of those a year, and I'm down to maybe 20 or 30 now. Some of that is just a by-product of spending more time in the software company, and some is just deciding there are audiences I want to be in front of and some that don't match the message I'm espousing.

But I love it. It's my retirement plan, candidly. I will always speak. I will always write another book and go out and promote the book and talk about it, because there's some dopamine hit from being on stage and connecting with an audience.

Julian: How do you get compensated? Do they pay you for this help as a consultant, or is it through products? How does that work?

Adam: It's a little bit of both. When I started out, it was just pure speaking-engagement fees, so I would get a speaking fee to come out and present. Then I realized the power of creating content, so I wrote books. I created audio programs and online courses. I did a documentary on student loan debt that we ended up selling to CNBC.

I consider myself a "mediapreneur", because I really like media. I like creating content and then turning around and selling it. It's a combination of me getting paid just to open my mouth and me getting paid to sell my wares, so to speak.

Julian: You don't actually deal with individual clients, then?

Adam: We do on the software side. We've got a number of subscribers for The Shred Method but nothing where I personally am working with clients.

Julian: With all your success, what's your biggest challenge right now?

Adam: I think my dad may have cursed me years ago. When I was in my early 20s, and I was trying to figure out what I wanted to do, he said, "Adam, your challenge will never be a lack of opportunity. Your challenge will be deciding which opportunity to pursue." It's been true.

There are so many cool opportunities to invest in. My challenge has been that I see one, and I get really excited for a period of time, and then I see something else, and I want to go after that. I made a commitment to one of my business partners that The Shred Method is the one thing we're going after, and we'll probably go after it for the next six or seven years with the hope of it becoming an acquisition target at some point.

As far as fintechs go, it will be a great business. There's a lot of data. Our clients are really solid. They're investors. They want to be investors. We think we're building a unique community, and right now, I'm committed to the success of that. My biggest challenge is keeping the blinders on.

Julian: What's your favorite investment today?

Adam: I love syndications. For a number of years, I was a real estate investor. I managed my own properties, and I was still building my speaking business at the time. My wife would say, "You're going over there again?" or, "You have to go to that house again? How much time did you spend over there?" It occurred to me that if I could invest in real estate and still get a K-1 and be treated like a partner but never have to set foot in another piece of real estate, that would be glorious.

When I was introduced to the whole syndication world, and I met a couple of syndication partners that I trust implicitly, I found my Nirvana investment, because I get great tax benefits and great income, and I never have to deal with tenants.

ADAM CARROLL IS AN INTERNATIONALLY RECOGNIZED FINANCIAL-LITERACY EXPERT AND LEADERSHIP-WORKSHOP FACILITATOR.

Adam has spent the past decade studying human behavior, particularly as it relates to personal leadership and personal finance.

He is the author of four Amazon bestsellers, a two-time TED talk speaker with nearly 6 million views on YouTube, and the creator of *Broke, Busted & Disgusted*, a documentary that aired on CNBC. He is the founder of The Shred Method, a cash-flow-management tool that is creating freedom for families everywhere.

Adam is passionate about helping people create financial freedom through unconventional financial strategies and modified habit patterns.

TO CONTACT ADAM

✉ hello@theshredmethod.com
🔗 https://www.theshredmethod.com/
https://www.adamspeaks.com/

CHAPTER 2

LIFE AFTER DEBT

Marcus Garrett

Julian: You host your own podcast, *Life After Debt*, where you talk about a variety of things, including how to brand yourself on social media. Why don't we start with the branding? That sounds very interesting.

Marcus: Recently, I've been focusing on YouTube, but I was most active on Instagram before that. I started in 2021, focusing on the brand *Life After Debt with The Marcus Garrett* and was able to scale from 2,000 followers to over 11,000. One of my favorite books that helped me bring it all together is *Key Person of Influence*, which talks about your Five-P System: your pitch, your product, your partnerships, your profile, and your publishing. For me, that was a book called *Debt Free or Die Trying*.

Julian: You've figured out a way to market yourself through social media.

Marcus: Yes, and I'm looking to monetize that over time. I had a guest on the show who calls it Phase Two. You build your brand to attract the audience, and then you monetize. He calls it the BAM System.

Julian: How do you get the audience? What's the trick to that?

Marcus: I've done it a number of ways. I've been in this space for 10 years, but my day job is as an auditor. That's why I like systems.

> I speak in systems a lot. I think a lot of people have dreams; they have goals, but they don't have a system to get them there.

As far as what's worked for me, I niched down into personal finance. 15 years ago, I was just blogging online like I think all senior millennials do. Then I started talking about wanting to improve my personal finances, which is a story you see everywhere now. That got some traction. I was already following the data because that was what I learned from my day job, and I said, "Okay, I think I have something here."

Ultimately, I pivoted into the personal-finance space, finding what was natural to me. I moved over to podcasts from a blog. Now it's all about short-form video with TikTok and Instagram, but I think it's leveraging the talents that you already have and then finding the spaces in which you can show off those talents and be successful. For me, it was Instagram. If you're younger, it might be TikTok or whatever comes next. I'm sure AI will be big in the next three-to-five years. If you're older, it might be Facebook or other social media or even print. Print still performs well.

Julian: When you say print, do you mean newspapers?

Marcus: Certainly. For example, I'm writing with Kiplinger now. My father used to give me Kiplinger magazines when I was in high school. It's all about determining where you want to meet your audience and then showing up to be successful.

Julian: What was the last article you wrote for Kiplinger?

Marcus: I think it was "11 Ways That You Can Use Your Graduation Money." On the back-end, we can answer any questions we want, and then the editors go through and choose which ones they want to promote and publish.

Julian: Got it. Tell me about the *Life After Debt*.

Marcus: That happened about a decade into the journey. I was already out of debt. When I wrote the book, I was chronicling my story from age 22 to age 30. I released the book at 31. I looked at the landscape and felt like the conversation just centered around debt.

> Everyone talks about debt management. Obviously, you have your traditional certified financial planners and financial advisors who are talking about investing and building wealth, but it seemed like most of it was about just accepting debt as a part of life. I said, "Well, what about life after debt? What if you want to get out of debt, or what if you want to do something beyond that?"

As I do when I don't see something out there, I created it myself and put a voice to it.

Julian: I assume you're talking about kids getting out of school with a lot of debt. Financial advisors tell them, "Give me your money to invest." But that's kind of hard when you don't have any money. In that case, what were some of the ideas you give people in debt? What were some of the things you taught?

Marcus: My system is a four-part system that's actually the second version of the book. I worked with the editor to help me improve and better tell the story. The first version was a chronological telling of my experiences from 22 to 30. The second version of the book is the system, because the editor said, "How do they replicate this? Chronology is important but not critical to their success." The second edition, D, defines the problem, which in most case is going to annualcreditreport.com, because...

> I think 60% of people don't even know how much debt they have. They don't know how much interest they're paying.

With that, you can, E, establish a plan, and that can go any number of different ways. I think the most popular is the debt snowball. For those who aren't familiar with that, it would be paying the lowest amount first and then snowballing towards the remainder of your debts, but I talked about three other systems as well. Once you've defined and established your plan, build a budget around that. One of my personal favorites happens to be 50-30-20, just because I'm an auditor. I like black and white lines to play within. But really, it's about the goal you want to accomplish and building a budget that will allow you to be successful. People ask me all the time, "What's the best system?" I answer, "The best system is the system that works." Finally, T, trust the process. *D-E-B-T-Debt-Free* is the title of the book.

Julian: Very interesting. You also talk about participation trophies. Can you tell us what those are?

Marcus: It doesn't come up as much anymore, but we're still building a generation on showing up rather than merit. I get the genesis behind that. We want all to succeed. But, as an elder or senior millennial, I still remember having to work. I ran track. I had to come in first, second, or third if I wanted to stand on the stage. I missed that participation-trophy timeline, and I guess I still have a chip on my shoulder about it. I still preach and practice walking the walk because if you want to succeed in life, you have to work for it. You have to put a system in place and be patient. That's why I dislike participation trophies.

Julian: You've been doing this for a while. What's something you wish you knew when you started?

Marcus:

> I wish I had invested sooner.

I just tackled the debt. Obviously, that plan was successful, but I did not realize I could have been concurrently investing. There was nothing stopping me. I just had this singular focus on getting out of debt. I didn't know about index funds. I didn't know about investments I could be making. I probably scratched the surface, but I didn't know I could go out and buy stocks. A quote I like says, "Teach the youth what you wish you had learned earlier." That would be something I wish I had learned earlier.

Julian: I agree schools should teach finance to students. It's crazy that they don't, but you obviously managed to find your own way even without that education. Now that you've achieved success, what's your biggest challenge going forward?

Marcus: I would say it would be defining what's next. If you were to take it by decades, in my 20s, I had my debt to tackle. In my 30s, I had my career to tackle. My father told me, "Use your 20s to learn, your 30s to apply, and your 40s to teach and mentor." I'm now in that next pivot of figuring out what teaching and mentoring looks like, and I think I've scratched the surface of it through the podcast and through the book, but I still have to figure out what my next race looks like.

I'm maybe one or two promotions away from the top of my career, yet I have 25 more years of work to do. I've been a division manager. I've been near director level, so there's probably assistant director and maybe director left for me, but I've got 25 more years of life to occupy, assuming a traditional retirement age of 65. What do those next 25 years look like? I don't think I'll be remembered for my amazing audit reports, so I'm looking at what my impact will be on the world.

Right now, as I said, I'm most active on YouTube. Although YouTube is 15 years old, I still think it'll be one of the platforms that stands the test of time. They have adapted well to all the changes, and you will be able to see me walk that journey in real time. I'm doing that through two forms. I have the traditional personal finance podcast, which is *Life After Debt with The Marcus Garrett*. My pitch there is to help working professionals who are struggling with burnout find easier or better ways to make and keep more money.

I think my next big thing will actually be a second channel I just launched called *How-To with The Marcus Garrett*. I take listener questions regarding debt and self-branding. I think that's what is next for me.

MARCUS GARRETT IS A MOTIVATIONAL SPEAKER, AUDITOR, AND BESTSELLING AUTHOR.

His book *D.E.B.T. Free or Die Trying: How I Buried Myself $30,000 in Debt and Dug My Way Out in 36-months on my way to an 800 FICO* is a #1 Amazon Kindle bestseller.

In addition to his speaking events, Marcus is the host of the podcast *Life After Debt with The Marcus Garrett*. He also appeared on many other podcasts and has written numerous articles.

TO CONTACT MARCUS

✉ marcus@themarcusgarrett.com

🔗 https://www.themarcusgarrett.com/

Part 2

GROWING YOUR MONEY

CHAPTER 3

MY INVESTMENT PHILOSPHY

Author Julian Rubinstein

E arlier in this book I shared a little about why I do things the way I do. Now I'd like to share some more information with you about my investment philosophy, and what our portfolios look like, so you can get a sense of what my clients experience.

Our portfolios are designed as target outcome investments. The portfolio is intended to provide investors with enhanced control over investment results with a predetermined amount of downside protection, upside participation and income with a specified maturity date. All our investments provide daily liquidity. Our portfolio aims to help investors concerned about market losses maintain market exposure.

> We provide investors with a buffer against market losses while still participating in the market's gains.

A major advantage of our portfolios is we are not concerned with daily fluctuations as every investment has a maturity date. When you have a maturity date it does not matter how the investment performs during the term. It only matters on the day the investment matures.

Our portfolios consist of four different types of investments, three for income and one for growth:

Income - This portion employs an option strategy on the S&P 500 that provides as much as 30% downside protection with the goal of providing annual income of 6-8% taxed at the long-term capital gain rate.

Income – This portion is invested in structured notes with a 50% downside barrier with the goal of providing 7-14% annual income.

Income – This portion is invested in short-term money market instruments, with the goal of earning 5% interest income and providing daily liquidity.

Growth – This portion is invested in the stock market and S&P 500, with up to 30% downside protection with upside potential of 8-19%.

We tailor the percentage of each investment to each client's goals & objectives.

I do not attempt to predict the future. I also do not listen to any of the pundits on CNBC who claim to know everything when in reality they know nothing. No one can predict what is going to happen with the stock market or the economy. Even if they could, they could never predict how people would react to that news. When North Korea detonated nuclear bombs, conventional wisdom would have been to sell stocks and buy bonds. Yet stocks rose. This is further proof that even if you can predict the future, you cannot predict how people will react.

That is why I follow what is called "rules-based investing". This is where you define a clear set of rules comprising an investment strategy. You stick to that strategy month after month regardless of your own emotions.

Developed through years of evolution, our basic human instincts are necessary for our survival. Keeping with the laws of the jungle, these instincts push us to run when in danger and charge when we see opportunity. The stock market, much like a casino, is built to take advantage of these instincts. Investors, if left to their primitive fear/greed instincts, tend to buy high and sell low.

These instincts harm their investing decisions. They make a naive person wait for a stock to double, triple, or even quadruple until every single person he knows claims to have made huge profits. Then he decides to buy, only to see the stock crash! What happens next to our hypothetical investor is that he looks at a 10% loss and hopes it will rebound. When the loss grows to 20%, he starts getting worried. At minus 27% he thinks of selling, but "Hey, this may be the bottom." When his loss hits 40%, he goes into shock and stops looking at the stock. When his loss reaches 60%, he gives up and stops checking his account. He feels he has been cheated and exits the markets. It may take years for him to return, if at all. Most likely, he will never recover his losses. Having downside protection for every investment prevents this from happening!

Strong opinions, like the ego, may also hinder an investor. Take the ordinary investor. This is especially true as we get older and feel wiser. A perfectly logical opinion goes like this. It is 2011 and interest rates are almost at zero. The average investor determines interest rates will rise in the future. (What else can they do?) So, the investor shorts the Treasuries. Eight years later long-term interest rates have barely moved, and our ordinary investor has once again lost money following his opinion.

Following rules prevents this process by eliminating ego and opinions. However, there are still biases at play, even when following a strategy. "How smart is my strategy? How smart am I for picking this strategy?" But these are easy to deal with. This is minimized by back testing and past performance.

> At the end of the day, the question should not be how smart I am, but rather how disciplined I am when the investment strategy dictates a buy and when it triggers a sell.

History shows that if you stay invested in the same strategy, you will probably make money. The challenge is to stick around. The more you get involved emotionally in the market, the quicker you will tire and give up. By following a rules-based strategy, you can spend less time watching the markets, reading news and analyses, and spend more time doing things you enjoy.

In the process, you will also improve your health. Because in investing, as in life, your most valued asset is time. The more you have the better your chances are.

CHAPTER 4

FINANCIAL PLANNING & DIVORCE

Robin Bresky

Julian: Why don't you tell us a bit about yourself and your practice?

Robin: I am an appellate attorney, and I've had my own practice for 22 years. Prior to that, I was a prosecutor in Broward County. Last May, I merged with a New York firm that goes by SSRGA. I came together with another boutique firm here in South Florida, and we opened the Florida office of SSRGA. We do family law and estate planning. We also do some real estate. In the family law arena, we do collaborative and litigation, and we are looking to expand our practice areas in the near future.

Julian: What attracted you to appellate law and family law?

Robin: The appellate portion of the practice is not only family law; it's all types of commercial litigation, civil and criminal. It's anything you could think of in the trial court. If there's an issue in the trial court and somebody is not happy, which often happens after a trial, they go to the next court higher, which, in Florida, is the appellate court or potentially the Florida Supreme Court or Federal Court. We do work in all of those arenas, and it's more of an academic practice because it's research and writing and oral argument versus a strategy at the trial level.

But to answer your question about family law, we do a number of family-law appeals, and that's just what happens to be very popular in Boca where our office is. Our litigation team also does family law, and they also do the collaborative if people are looking to work together instead of litigate. It's a very unique and interesting way to settle a dissolution of marriage.

Julian: Does collaborative happen after a bad judgment or before?

Robin: That would be before. In the collaborative process, each party gets their own attorney, but they agree to collaborate and share experts. While it's not my area of the law, it doesn't actually go to litigation. They agree to come together and decide that they're going to determine how to work it out amongst themselves with the help of a therapist and perhaps a forensic accountant. They share the experts rather than each of them getting their own expert. If for any reason the collaborative process breaks down and they have to go to litigation, they have to start all over with new attorneys because the attorneys are prohibited from litigating because they're sharing information willingly rather than going to court and paying each time for a motion to get discovery. That's why it's a collaborative process.

Julian: What would you say is the biggest financial mistake people make after divorce?

Robin: From an appellate perspective, you can appeal anything that has a good faith basis, but you really want to look at the likelihood of success on that, because...

> sometimes people want to keep fighting and, depending on the situation, it could be costly.

If it doesn't go their way, they could think of it as a mistake, obviously.

Before the divorce, I think it's just the problem with the dissolution and also in the guardianship arena. It's a very emotional case, and emotions tend to drive it. In things having to do with family in general, those issues are more emotional, and even if the parties themselves have very good business sense, sometimes it's hard to prevail. I think that might be the issue.

Julian: That makes sense. What have you seen from people that get divorced as far as financial planning goes? Do they do intelligent planning before divorce? Do they handle it right post-divorce?

Robin: They certainly should redo their estate plans, and...

> we advocate that they redo their estate plans even while they're in the midst of the divorce, because God forbid something happens to one of the

> parties during the divorce. If they're not yet divorced and they don't have a will, for example, it's all going to go to their spouse because they're not yet divorced.

Of course, every situation is individual, but we do think it makes sense for each party to have their own financial planner and CPA, and we try to bring that all in together to get the right resources to our clients so they can benefit from having as many resources as possible. Of course, it depends on the size of the assets and what they're dealing with. Every situation, as I said, is very unique.

Julian: As a family-law attorney, is there anything that surprises you? You probably have seen everything.

Robin: I've seen a lot, but I tend to be continually surprised about things. When you think you've seen it all, then you realize you haven't.

Julian: What aspect of your firm do you think people underutilize?

Robin: Not to be repetitive, but it may be the estate planning, because people tend to put off things which they don't think are necessary right away.

> If you are going through a dissolution of marriage, it's important to get a new estate plan in place, and I think that might be underutilized from those particular clients.

Julian: What mistakes do you think the non-working spouse makes when it comes to financial planning? During the divorce or afterward. Do you think it's important that they have a financial planner during divorce?

Robin: I think it is helpful. The non-working spouse may decide they want to keep the house, and then they have a mortgage so they can only stay in the house for a certain amount of time before they realize they have to sell the house. I definitely think a financial planner can be beneficial during the process to advise the client on what really is in their best interest with regards to what sort of settlement they're looking to get or what they will be able to support themselves with moving forward. The biggest mistake the non-working spouse makes is continuing not to work, potentially.

Julian: Having been divorced, it is a very unusual practice of law because, as you say, there's a lot of emotion in it. It's not just cut-and-dry. Business litigation is a lot easier because cooler heads prevail.

Robin: Absolutely. When you're doing litigation in a business context, you're just looking at the bottom line. Even if you're looking at whether or not to bring the lawsuit or defend the lawsuit or settle, you're just looking for the most cost-effective way to resolve this. That is not typically what's at the forefront when emotion takes over. It's difficult to have that part of the brain prevail, especially at the outset.

ROBIN I. BRESKY IS A PARTNER IN THE FLORIDA OFFICE OF SCHWARTZ SLADKUS REICH GREENBERG ATLAS LLP.

Robin focuses her practice on appellate law and litigation support for civil, commercial, personal injury, family law, and criminal matters.

She received her Juris Doctor from Chicago-Kent College of Law and her Bachelor of Science degree from the University of Florida. Prior to joining SSRGA, Robin owned her own boutique firm in Boca Raton, Florida that focused on appeals, trusts and estates and corporate transactions. She started her legal career as a prosecutor in the Broward State Attorney's Office.

Robin is past president of the National Conference of Women's Bar Associations, a fellow of the American Bar Association, and since 2001, a member of the Appellate Judges Conference. As a passionate advocate for women's rights, she served as president of the Florida Association for Women Lawyers (FAWL) and president of the South Palm Beach County chapter. Her firm does pro bono work and raises money for the Legal Aid Society of Palm Beach County.

TO CONTACT ROBIN

✉ rbresky@breskyappellate.com
🔗 https://ssrga.com/

CHAPTER 5

FINDING THE 'PERFECT FIT' FRANCHISE

Marty Greenbaum

Julian: Why don't you start by telling us about your company and what you do?

Marty: I am founder and owner of Smart Franchise Investing. I've been in franchising over 30 years and started my career in a franchising family, opening business and postal centers. Some people may be aware of a brand called PostNet. They're like UPS stores. When I was 28 years old, I left PostNet and started a marketing company to follow my passion for marketing. I was a marketing strategist in franchising, very active in the International Franchise Association, and helped over 120 franchise brands. For most of my career, I was a business owner focused on helping franchise companies grow. My specialty was franchise development, basically helping franchises find great franchise owner candidates. Five years ago, I decided I'd had enough of the marketing business and the traveling and I became what they call a franchise consultant, helping people learn about franchising and find that "perfect fit" franchise.

Most people just don't understand franchising other than their experiences as a customer. If I ask someone to name a franchise, they're going to say Chick-fil-A, McDonald's, or even Krispy Kreme. The fact is...

> there are 3,500 franchises out there, and there are some great ones, but not all are great and not all are the right fit for a lot of people.

I help people learn about franchising and identify the franchises that are best suited to help them achieve their goals.

Julian: What's the first step someone should take if they're looking to buy a franchise?

Marty: First of all, franchises are awarded. It used to be that if you had the money and you had a heartbeat, they would sell you a franchise. Nowadays, they're looking for great operators and people that are driven to succeed. You have to be the right fit for a franchise organization. Most people go online and start doing some research and randomly reach out to those franchises they have heard about are tied into things they know or skills they have. Maybe they were a customer of a franchise. Maybe they had a good friend that did really well on a certain type of franchise. Maybe they read an article or a story. Those are the things that drive people to franchising.

Most people say, "Why would I want to franchise when I can open my own business?" I'll give you a quick hint:

> Because 80% of business owners will fail in the first five years. Franchising has a much higher

success rate, often two-to-three times that of independent business owners. It makes sense to go in on a franchise, as long as you select the right franchise.

But for most people, they look online, they fill out a bunch of forms, and they get a million salespeople calling them to sell them franchises. If you've never owned a business or bought a franchise in the past, how are you going to tell what's good and what's not, who's giving it to you straight and who's being a little misleading?

These are the problems that people run into when they first jump into this franchising world.

Julian: How do people determine the right franchise for them?

Marty: First of all, I think you've got to begin by assessing your long-term goals and how you're going to reach them. If you have a great job and you don't want to leave your job, could you own a franchise? Yes, you can. There are owner-operator franchises and there are semi-absentee franchises. You could keep your job and be a semi-absentee franchise owner. More and more people are working a hybrid schedule, where they'll work several days a week at home and many of them are working from home every day of the week. They're able to keep their primary careers and create some flexibility in their schedules to have a manager in place and manage the manager. Nowadays, semi-absentee franchises are more prevalent than ever.

If you're serious about franchising then I recommend you take stock in where you're at in your career, how much time you really have, and determine if this something you can afford to do. There are franchises at every price range, you could get into a franchise for as low as $100,000, and they go up from there.

There are what they call "brick and mortar" franchises, places where you get your car serviced, get a haircut, get food, get a massage, and so much more. Because you have a location, and you're signing a lease, those tend to run $300,000-to-$600,000. Those are bigger investments because you have a buildout of the space, equipment, signs, and more expenses

There are service franchises, where you're going to someone's house or business to repair something or provide a service. These include things like carpet cleaning, painting, remodeling, plumbing, HVAC, pest control, blind installation, lawn care, and so many more.

Home-service franchises are hot, but your investments are going to be much lower than in retail—generally $100,000 to $200,000. Service franchises are more affordable, but there are other attributes you need to consider. Definitely take stock on how much time you have. Take a look at investment levels and really determine your goals.

We're all on this path in life. Most of us didn't really choose that path. It's not always a master plan. We get on a path. We're doing pretty well. We stay on that path. But at some point, you look at that path and say, "You know what? If I'm going to retire with X, am I going to be comfortable? Can I support my family? What if something comes up?"

We don't know what's happening in this world. Take stock in where you're at and where you need to be and set better goals for yourself. Sometimes you have to get off that path and start a new path, and that may be finding a business that could supplement what you're doing so you're saving quicker, gaining more ground, and building your wealth. Franchising could do that.

In franchising, you're not putting money in the market and crossing your fingers. You have a little more control over it. Those are things to consider when you're looking at making a move and finding some type of franchise investment.

Julian: Can you give us an example of a hands-off type of franchise where you're just the investor?

Marty: There are very few fully hands-off franchises, but I'll share with you some deep models. There's a pet-grooming franchise. Pet grooming is really big right now, and so is delivery service. Think of all the food companies that bring food to you, DoorDash and all these food companies. Why wouldn't you want to have your pet groomed in your driveway? This company has state-of-the-art vans, and they come groom your pet at your house.

It's hands-off. But even better than that, the franchisor has a management team that manages the franchise for you. They hire your general manager and your staff. They manage the marketing. They manage the budgets. Twice a month, you review and make decisions on whom you're going to hire or fire, what expenses you have to make, what marketing you want to do. That's the ultimate hands-off. But there are different levels of semi-absentee, depending on how much time you have and where your interests are.

Julian: Right now, hiring seems to be very difficult. In the franchise world, is it just as difficult?

Marty: Oh, yes. There are areas of the country where it's a bit tougher than others. There are certain franchises that, because of their business models, are still able to attract great workers. They're competitive in their ability to pay. But food service is still kind of a tough space. When most people think of franchises, they're thinking of food service. But there are so many other options: healthcare, senior care, IT, the pet industry, automotive, education.

Julian: Got it. Are there any franchises that are considered recession-proof?

Marty: Definitely. If your pipe breaks at home right now, and we're in a recession, are you going to not have it fixed?

There are so many senior-care agencies right now, especially in Florida. There are tons of seniors. Senior-care agencies are pretty recession-proof. There is a rise in the demand for senior care because more baby boomers are turning older every day.

Automotive is another one. If your car breaks down, it doesn't matter if there's a recession; you're going to fix it. Then, there's home services. Right now, because the high interest rates make it tough to buy, people are fixing up their houses.

Julian: What is a mistake that most franchisees make that's very hard to undo?

Marty: They rush to buy a franchise without having all the information. Once you buy a franchise, it's a 10-year agreement. It's like getting married. If you don't do the due diligence, you could really be putting your investment at risk.

When people don't know about the financial industry, they go to an expert. If they don't know the real estate market, they go to an expert. But for some reason, a lot of people will still go directly to the franchisors.

Franchise salespeople are really good. They know how to spin things. The problem is, it's a mixed bag out there. You don't know what you're going to get. Before you buy, you want to talk to other franchisees and validate whether it is a great franchise system or not.

> If I was buying into a franchise, I would reach out to as many franchisees in the system as possible and say, "How are you doing? What kind of money are you making? If you had the choice to redo this decision, would you?" Visit locations, talk to franchisees, hire an attorney. Before you sign a franchise agreement, get with an attorney and make sure you know what you're getting into.

Find out how they get customers. Marketing is one of the hardest things. Great franchisors have that figured out for you. I like the franchises that have a very strong marketing-and-lead-generation strategy. Things like that are very important. Technology could be a deal breaker. Even painting companies nowadays have a fair amount of tech. You can plug in the measurements to each room and get a bid right there with the customer, which also tells you exactly how much paint you have to have for the job. For a roofing franchise, there are drones that measure the roof.

Those things are all going to be important when you're looking at franchises because, if you're paying a royalty for 10 years on all your sales, it's about the value you get. "How do I get the most value for the royalties I'm paying?" That should be your mindset.

Julian: So, you walk people through this process?

Marty: I do a couple of things. I educate them about franchising, and I have a process to help them identify which franchises could be best suited for them based on who they are, their skills, their goals, and how much money they want to spend.

We talk about all these different variables, and I learn about them. I'm going to make some recommendations based on this process. Then, based on what my clients like, I connect them with the brands. They have discussions with those select brands, and I'm there to guide them, answer questions, and lend perspective to what they're learning.

Julian: Is it a set fee for the service, or does it depend on each case?

Marty: Actually, it's free. I know that's going to sound odd, but it's free to my clients, kind of like real estate. When you're buying a house, the buyer doesn't pay the agent commission; the seller does. If someone decides to move forward with a franchise that I made a recommendation on, and they've done all their due diligence, then I would receive a referral fee from the franchise company that would not affect what my client would pay.

I'm about no pressure. I'm straight-up. I want people to succeed. This is a big decision for anybody going into business, and you can't afford to make a bad decision. I'm definitely here to help.

Julian: With all your success, what's your biggest challenge?

Marty: My biggest challenge is I want to continue to grow this business and find great people. I love to spread the word, saying, "Hey, there are some options out there that maybe you don't know about." My other big challenge is staying on top of the mountains of information I have to learn about all these specific franchises.

Everything's constantly changing, and I stay up to date on all of it. I'm always reading emails and other content to make sure I'm as good as I can be for my clients.

Julian: What sets you apart from your competition? What makes you unique?

Marty: I was a business owner and a marketing strategist for over 27 years, so I'm very analytical. I worked on the other side. I had franchisors as clients. I spoke at franchising conferences. I was at hundreds of events. I have very deep roots in franchising. My family started a franchise organization.

I don't think you'll find many consultants that have the depth of knowledge and experience in franchising that I have. I have been through those challenges or struggles. I take this very seriously. That's how I'm a little bit different than most in doing what I do.

MARTY GREENBAUM, CFE IS A 30+ YEAR FRANCHISE-INDUSTRY PROFESSIONAL, AND THE FOUNDER OF SMART FRANCHISE INVESTING.

 Marty has been involved in opening 500 stores, serving as Director of Operations and ultimately as Vice President of Marketing. He launched and operated a prestigious franchise-marketing agency that served over 120 franchise brands and earned the distinction of Certified Franchise Executive (CFE) from the International Franchise Association (IFA).

Marty has been a speaker at franchise-industry events, a supplier member of the IFA, and a franchising advocate on Capitol Hill. Today, he serves motivated investors seeking to reach their personal and financial goals through franchise ownership.

TO CONTACT MARTY

✉ marty@smartfranchiseinvesting.com

🔗 https://www.smartfranchiseinvesting.com/

CHAPTER 6

DEFINE WHERE YOU ARE GOING

Rocky Lalvani

Julian: You're interesting because you're doing something I've really never heard of. Can you tell us a bit about yourself and your business?

Rocky: I am basically a profit expert. I work with small-business owners to help them with their finances inside their businesses. I've always been a personal-money nerd. From the time I was young, I was always investing and building up my wealth. I am an immigrant. When we came here, we started with very little. I was amazed that more states weren't wealthy. As I started to look around, I realized there were a couple of reasons for that. One was money mindsets. How are you going to get good with money if it's a taboo subject?

I assumed people who went into business understood the business of business, and...

I was shocked to learn that most business owners weren't looking at their financials at all. They weren't looking at their accounting. Many of them just did not enjoy it at all.

I'm sure, as a financial planner, you really realize if you don't look at your numbers, you're going to make a mess of them. I partnered with Mike Michalowicz, who wrote the book *Profit First*. We work with small-business owners to change the way they look at numbers and to change their entire mindsets about how they spend.

Julian: Can you give us some examples of some people you've worked with and what you've done for them?

Rocky: Sure, but first, let's talk about how Mike changed the equation. We're all told sales minus expenses equals profit, which means profit is a leftover. Mike said, "Wait a minute. We're supposed to pay ourselves first, right? Why don't we say, 'sales minus profit equals expenses'"? You pay yourself first, just like on the personal side. If you want to build wealth, take the money out of your check before you even see it so you can't spend it. Automate all of your finances so your money is going to building wealth. It's the same thing in business.

> This system basically automates the business finances. It gives every dollar a job, and it sends it to do that job, whether it's profit, the owner's paycheck, or it goes towards paying the owner's taxes. The rest goes to pay for their operating expenses. What they're doing is constraining their spending. If you want to go on a diet, you get a smaller plate. If you have a smaller plate, you eat less. If you have a smaller bank account, you spend less. People will spend all the money they have. It's lifestyle inflation.

The same thing happens inside of a business. The more money you have, the more you tend to spend. You get a little bit lazy with it. The business owners I tend to work with are the ones who are allergic to looking at their financials. They want someone to look at their financials, read the tea leaves, and tell them what's going on. I think that's one of the biggest problems for business owners. The P&L tells part of the story. The balance sheet tells another part of the story. The cash flow report tells another part of the story. But there's no one thing that gives them the total story. The other problem is all of those are in the rearview mirror. I am sure you probably say to people that past returns don't predict future results.

Your old reports aren't going to tell you what to do tomorrow. What we really try to do is help the business owners see what's going on in the moment and predict the future as best they can. Once you put a bit of attention to this, your ability to have cash flow to make wiser decisions is just a natural outcome.

We've had business owners who were in business for over 10 years and always struggled. Generally within about 18 months, they invariably say to me, "We've never had so much cash in the business. What do we do?" I tell them, "Take the money out of your business. Give it to someone like Julian and build wealth outside your business, because you never know when the economy's going to hit a recession. Make sure you're building another stream of income or safety somewhere else outside the business." For a lot of business owners, removing money from the company is a struggle. Paying themselves is a struggle. They're always taking care of everyone else before themselves.

Julian: You're saying that by knowing they're going to pay themselves first and they have a limited amount of money to spend elsewhere, they're going to think long and hard about how they spend that money.

Rocky: Correct. They're going to better manage their cash flow because, too often, we throw money at problems instead of being resourceful. But when they're forced to be resourceful, business owners do amazing things. You've got to constrain them. You've got to hold them back from throwing money at every problem, because more often than not, we waste it.

Julian: That's very interesting. I definitely could see how that is a problem. You spend so much money on expenses and advertising, you forget to pay yourself.

Rocky: Yes, and when you paid the advertising bill that was supposed to be your paycheck, you feel all right because you're told to reinvest in your business. Everyone's constantly told to reinvest in their businesses. When are you actually going to get a payout from your business? Has that been planned? Do you know what it is? Large companies all have CFOs. There is somebody at the helm looking at their financials. In most small businesses, that's not the case. The accountant and the bookkeeper don't know how to do this. They're not sitting in that CFO chair. They're sitting in the tax-compliance chair to make sure the numbers are all correct. They really can't help the business owner, and the business owner doesn't even understand what they're talking about.

Julian: They're not seeing the big picture.

Rocky: Correct.

Julian: If there was just one thing you could share with every client, what would that be?

Rocky: First of all, if you're a business owner reading this, and you think I'm crazy, what we tell people is to take one small step.

> Set up one bank account that's separate, designate it, and call it your profit account. Every month take 1% of your sales and put it in that account. You will not miss a dollar out of a hundred. Once you start to see how much money that 1% is over time, and it's not hurting you, make it 2%.

This is the same thing as personal finance. Start saving and slowly increase it, and over time, it's not going to be hard to get to a five or 10% profit margin, because over that time, you're going to constrain yourself and go through all your expenses and say, "Where are we wasting money in our business?" Just like people at home have this subscription service and that subscription service, in business, that goes on steroids: "Oh, I signed up for this trial and I haven't used it. My employee signed up for this software and we stopped using it six months ago. I'm paying for three different services that do the same thing." It's all about being aware of what's going on in your business, constraining yourself, and automating your profit.

Julian: I always marvel at how many of these automated subscriptions people have, and they just forget about them.

How much money do these companies make because people just forget that they have the subscription?

Rocky: Not to mention they raise the price every year.

Julian: Right, like people who pay for Gmail; an employee leaves, they forget to cancel the Gmail account, and they're paying for it forever.

Rocky: Often, I'll ask people, "Why are you paying so much for a Gmail account? Why do you have the top-tier Gmail when all you need is the bottom-tier Gmail?"

I was paying for this one subscription service that was only nine bucks a month. I didn't care that much. But I finally said, "I think I'm done with this." I went to cancel it, and it actually showed me the total I paid. It was $270. How did $9 turn into 270? It was so inconsequential, but this stuff multiplies. It compounds. The key is to get on the right side of the compounding.

Julian: Businessmen tell me, "Make sure you look after the pennies because the dollars look after themselves." Big expenses you're going to notice. It's the little ones that you don't notice, and that's what kills you, because they add up. You've got to pay attention to the small things.

Rocky: It depends on the business model. I know these days everyone thinks selling on the internet is so easy. You start looking at these e-commerce models and the platform fees, and it is pretty scary how much all those platforms are charging, which is why they're all big and filthy rich. A small business owner is struggling because, between their cost of goods and their platform fees, and advertising, they literally make pennies. If they're not managing those pennies, they're in serious trouble.

Julian: What's the one mistake almost everyone makes?

Rocky: I'll tell it more like a story. You go to the airport. You get on the plane. The pilot comes on and says, "Hey, I don't know where we're going today, and I don't know if they put fuel in the tank." Are you going to stay on that airplane? Business owners don't define where they're going. Where are you going to be on December 31st of this year? What will your sales be? What are your expenses going to be? What's the budget? How much cash do you need to get from here to there? If you don't know how much cash you need halfway through the year, you might run out of cash.

Everyone wants to sell into these big places like Costco or Sam's Club. But if I want to sell something to Costco, I have to go buy all the materials, and then I have to produce it. That all takes cash. Then I have to ship it to Costco. Costco still hasn't paid me. They're probably not going to pay me for 120 days. 75 days later, they call me and say, "We love your stuff. Send me another order." Now, I'm paying for a second set of materials, second set of employee work, second set of shipping, and I still don't have a dollar coming in my door.

If you don't know how to pay for the cash flow of growth, you will find yourself in trouble. I think most business owners just say, "If I sell more, it will all fix itself." No. One of the biggest reasons businesses fail is they grow too fast, and they don't have the cash to get them through the growth.

Julian: I have a piece of art in my office that says, "If you don't know where you want to go, you never know how to get there."

Rocky: Exactly. If you ask people what they want, I don't think most people can define that answer. The same goes for the business owner. What do you want? Where are you going?

> If we know where we're going and what we want, it becomes really easy to ignore shiny objects. It becomes easy to reverse engineer the path to get there, even on the personal-retirement side.

When do you want to retire? How much money do you want to retire with? Once you know those numbers, it becomes very easy to do the math. Then the bigger question is, what do you want to do when you retire? If you just retire, you probably go off and die. You need to have a meaningful purpose.

Julian: I tell everyone, "Retirement is really not the pot of gold at the end of the rainbow. You can be bored to death." Everyone says, "Oh, no, I'll play golf. I'll play tennis. I'll keep busy." I have so many clients who retired early and would pay someone for a job.

Rocky: What I do now is my retirement business. I do what I love. I don't do what I don't want to do. I have fun, and I make more money than I did when I was working.

I planned it. I said, "This is what I want from life. This is what I want to do. This is who I want to help. Now, let me just reverse engineer what I need to do to make that happen." It's not just money; it's time. It's constraints on time as well. It's constraints on money. The one thing people don't value is their time. They don't realize how precious it is and how little they have of it.

Julian: That's a famous Mark Cuban comment, right? The only thing money cannot buy is time.

Rocky: Correct, and the same thing goes for the business owner. You have to value the time. Years ago, you would hear people say this. They would sell books on eBay that they would get for free, and they still lost money because they didn't value the amount of time it would take to create a listing, put it in the box, go to the post office, and ship the stuff out. When they started looking at their actual time, they were making pennies an hour. It wasn't worth the effort.

More often than not, we don't know what our time is worth. If I know what my time is worth, I can get rid of tasks I don't want to do. If my time is worth $200 an hour, I'm not mowing the lawn. I'm paying some guy $40 or $50 to do it. The same goes for other parts of life. But that doesn't mean I pay somebody $50 to mow my lawn, and I go watch a Netflix movie. I'm out generating income. This way, I don't have to spend time over here doing the things I might not enjoy. If you love cutting the lawn, cut the lawn. That's fine. But you've got to know what you want.

Julian: How do you define success?

Rocky:

Success is the ability to do what you want when you want, the ability to say yes and no.

Julian: I like that. With all the success you have had, what is your biggest challenge today?

Rocky: That's a good question. I'll put it a little bit more generally. Most people want to change the world and do all these big things. I'm just trying to change myself. It's more about self-development, I think. How do I find peace no matter what happens?

You get in a car accident. Can you be peaceful? Your plane is late. Can you be peaceful? Somebody didn't do what you wanted them to. Can you be peaceful?

Julian: You have two podcasts. Talk about them.

Rocky: One is *Richer Soul* and the other is *Profit Answer Man*. On *Profit Answer Man*, we teach business owners how to be profitable. On *Richer Soul*, we ask "Once you're profitable, how do you live the ultimate life? How do you live a life of harmony?" People try to live a life of balance. You can't live a life of balance, because life will never be in perfect balance. But how do you live a life of harmony? How do you figure out how different parts of life come and go? How do you play the music you want to play for your life and enjoy it? That's a big part of what we talk about there: mindset, purpose, setting your goals. Then, how do you look at all the components of life, from health to wealth to time to relationships to spirituality? How do you create all of that for you?

> The biggest thing that holds people back is taking the first step. It's the hardest part. Take the first step, and the rest will follow.

But you can't steer a ship in port. You've got to get moving. Just take the tiniest step and then take the next one and keep trying. When you have a target, it becomes much either easier to define the next step.

ROCKY LALVANI SERVES AS CHIEF PROFITABILITY ADVISER FOR BUSINESS OWNERS.

 As a certified Profit First Professional, Rocky implements Mike Michalowicz's Profit First System.

The child of first-generation immigrants, Rocky started with nothing. In spite of his early struggles, and his mom passing away when he was seven, he has been able to achieve financial success. Rocky loves to share his journey and inspire others to achieve their dreams.

TO CONTACT ROCKY

rocky@lalvani.net
https://profitcomesfirst.com/
https://richersoul.com/

Part 3

RETIREMENT AND ASSET PROTECTION

CHAPTER 7

ACCESSING FINANCES FOR LONG-TERM CARE

Howard Krooks

Julian: You're a partner at the law firm Cozen O'Connor. Tell us a bit about you and your practice.

Howard: I'm an attorney who practices in elder law and estate planning in New York, Florida, and Pennsylvania. I have been doing this for over 30 years and really enjoy the ability to work with people to help plan their estates and achieve asset protection in the face of government benefits. We handle guardianship-type proceedings, special-needs planning, Medicaid planning, veterans-benefits planning—a wide variety of issues that affect the elderly and people with disabilities.

Julian: What exactly is Medicaid planning? I'm sure most people don't even know what it is, and I've learned that it's a very important thing for people to understand, especially as they get older.

Howard: Medicaid planning has to do with accessing through government benefit programs, financing for the cost of long-term care. People either self-finance, which means they have very high net worths, or they've got to look towards Medicare, which really doesn't pay for very much in the way of long-term care services. People are very surprised to learn that their Medicare coverage is limited in that regard. If they don't have a high net worth, and if they are not going to be able to rely on Medicare, there are limited sources of financing.

They're going to have to either exhaust their small amount of assets, or they're going to need a long-term care insurance policy in place, or they can look to another government benefit program known as Medicaid. Medicaid is the only government program that truly does pay for long-term custodial care, whether it be at home, in an assisted living facility or in a nursing home. When you look at nursing home costs, generally speaking, they run $10,000 to $12,000 a month in the South Florida area, $14,000 to $18,000 in New York, and somewhere in between in Pennsylvania.

> You're looking at very exorbitant costs for custodial care, around the clock care, and most people find that they either cannot afford it, or if they can for some period of time, it would result in either partial or full exhaustion of whatever assets they do have, preventing them from taking a lifetime of savings and being able to pass that on to their kids or a surviving spouse. Medicaid planning says, "What can we do to plan our estate so that we can both qualify for government benefits and protect some of those assets?"

Julian: How do you go about protecting your assets to still get the coverage?

Howard: Well, each state has its own rules. What we talk about today has to be taken with that in mind. Whatever I say might apply in one state but not in another state. Each state has rules that govern the disposition of assets, and certain asset transfers are going to result in a disqualifying period where, if you've made the asset transfer, you'll not qualify for Medicaid. Other asset transfers are acceptable and legitimate, and you can engage in them without erasing your eligibility for Medicaid.

We as attorneys help educate our clients and implement a plan that is within the parameters of acceptable planning as outlined in these regulations. For example, in Florida, if you own what's called income-producing real estate, Medicaid will not count it as an asset. You can protect assets by purchasing income-producing real estate and still qualify for government benefits. You just have to know the ins and outs of how that works. But if you know this is a possible planning opportunity, you're going to avail yourself of that opportunity. You can have your cake and eat it too, so to speak, because the asset can be protected, yet you're still qualifying for Medicaid, and you're remaining within the parameters of the Medicaid eligibility requirements of your state.

Julian: But does the government take the income from the property?

Howard: In that case, yes, they will take the income. If you had $200,000 in assets, and the Medicaid asset limit is $2,000, you could purchase a real estate property for $200,000 and take that asset off the table. That income will have to be used towards the cost of your care, but most people are comforted by the fact that they save the principal and they can pay the income towards their care, but at least they protected the asset.

Julian: Let's assume it throws off $10,000 of income. You're saying the government will pick up the other $100,000?

Howard: Well, let's take out our calculators for a second, because if you're throwing out $10,000 of income, how much principal are we talking about? Fair-market-value rent is somewhere around 3.5%, so if you're throwing off that much income, you have enough assets that you can pay for your long-term care on the income alone.

Julian: If you have a $200,000 property, at 3.5%, that would be $7,000 of income. Would you still qualify?

Howard: Yes, you'd still qualify. You would have to use the $7,000 spread out over 12 months. That becomes an increase to your monthly income, but the $200,000 is noncountable, and when you pass away, it goes to your heirs.

Julian: That's the first time I've ever heard of that.

Howard: There are other planning opportunities. For example, oftentimes there is a family caregiver. The caregiver doesn't necessarily want to get paid because they're doing it out of love and affection. But if you are providing extensive caregiving, you can actually get paid to do that because it's pursuant to a written personal-care contract, which is accepted by Medicaid. When you transfer money, instead of it disqualifying you, you can take the position that it is payment and compensation for those services that are being rendered. That is a legitimate way to move assets over to another family member without jeopardizing your eligibility.

Julian: That's very interesting. I think what you're trying to get at primarily is that you can qualify for government assistance without going broke first.

Howard: That's right. Wherever you're situated, whatever state you're in, you're going to want to consult with somebody who's expert in the rules of that state, because they're going to know all of the nuances of qualifying and the traps for the unwary. Make sure you get your planning in place and make sure you do it right. But what you said is absolutely correct; there are ways you can both qualify for Medicaid and preserve assets. You've just got to know what you're doing.

Julian: Is there ever a way to get coverage for in-home care?

Howard: There is. There are some obstacles depending upon your state, again. For example, in New York, there's no wait period. There's no wait list for home care services. In addition, you're more likely to get 24/7 caregiving in New York than you are in a state like Florida. Florida does have a wait list. Sometimes that wait period could be several weeks. It could be several months, and it could even be upwards of a year, which is very challenging to navigate because you need care now. That's a challenge in Florida that doesn't exist in New York. But having said that, is home care available in Florida? Yes, it is. You've just got to know how to navigate those waters.

Julian: But you're saying you could end up paying for an entire year, which could become impossible.

Howard: Right, and sometimes people make sacrifices. They don't get the care they need. We have what's called an institutional bias in our Medicaid system. Even though someone might be a good candidate to receive services in their home, they're forced into the nursing home because states are not allowed to impose a wait period for nursing home Medicaid. On the one hand, you'd rather stay home and go on the wait list, but you can't wait a year, so in order to get the needed services today, you simply opt for the program that allows you to get those services immediately. The only program that does that is the skilled nursing facility level of care. They're forced into the nursing home just to get the care they need now.

Julian: I assume you can't get on the list until you have less than $2,000 of assets.

Howard: Well, technically that's not true. You can get on the list. It's just that once you are called off the wait list, they give you about 30 days to submit your financial documentation, which they will then review. If at that point you still have more than $2,000 in assets, you would be declined and not approved. But you can use that 30-day period to do the planning that's necessary. By the time you submit the financial documentation, you must have engaged in planning so that you meet the Medicaid asset limit.

Julian: Very interesting. I know you also do a lot of work in estate planning, and we've talked about rule-based planning versus revocable-trust-based planning. Can you touch on that?

Howard: Absolutely. Most people think of estate planning as involving a will, and if you suggest a trust, they may think, "I don't have enough assets for a trust, and I don't want to get involved." But there are some advantages to doing trust-based planning over a will-based plan. What's the difference?

> In a will-based plan, you just have a will. That's your testamentary document. That's where all your wishes are contained as to what is to happen with your assets when you pass away. A revocable-trust-based plan uses both a trust and a will. They work in conjunction with each other, and most of your wishes are contained in the trust document. The reason people opt for the trust instead of just a will-based plan is that if you become incapacitated, having your assets in the trust is better than just having a will.

With just a will, you only have a power of attorney that allows somebody else to manage your assets. Often, through the passage of 10 or 20 years since you signed the power of attorney, banks and financial institutions may not know who the agent is that's appointed under the power of attorney. When they walk into the branch to use that power of attorney, there are a lot of challenges to getting it honored. But if you set up a trust, at the time you set up the trust, you're providing a copy of the document to the financial institution. They have it on record since day one of the account being opened, and it provides a more seamless transition of supervision and management of the assets in the trust than if you only had a will.

Asset management is one of the benefits. The other benefit that serves as a primary reason why people do a trust-based plan is probate avoidance. Probate is not the enemy that a lot of people think it is. We do probate all the time, and it's really not that big a deal. Having said that, if you own a piece of real estate, and you want your heirs to be able to deal with that real estate, they're going to have an easier time doing that if you used a trust-based plan than if you did just a will. A will has to go through probate, and a trust does not. The probate process can take several months.

Maybe someone wants to buy the property in the estate, but if it's still in probate, you may lose the buyer. If it was in the trust, the trustee has the authority to immediately dispose of the property in furtherance of preserving a trust asset and converting it into liquid cash. You will not have to go through probate in order to effectuate that kind of sale. You can also arrange for much sooner distributions from a trust than from a will. It just streamlines everything.

Julian: In our firm, we have a client going through probate now, and the IRA is supposed to be passing right to the heirs, but the bank is not accepting the power of attorney. We learned that if the POA doesn't specifically state you can change an IRA beneficiary, then you cannot do it.

Howard: Let me speak to that. Florida's power-of-attorney law was changed in 2011. Florida's legislature determined that general clauses in a power of attorney were not going to be valid in Florida, so if you say something like, "My agent has the authority to do anything and everything that I could do," that's meaningless in a Florida power of attorney. They've determined that if you're going to give authority to somebody, you need to be specific. You've got to make sure anything you want your agent to be able to do is spelled out in language that clearly communicates the authority. You just can't use a catchall phrase.

Some people don't know that. In this day and age, you've got your internet-based powers of attorney, and they come up with this generic form you can download and use in any state you want, but it's not going to work in Florida. If you didn't know that, you may have thought you did something good by at least having that document signed, but the execution requirements may not be valid, and you may not be compliant with Florida specificity requirements. You've got to be really careful with internet-based forms.

Julian: We had a case where the power of attorney was created in 2009, and we're still fighting with TD Ameritrade to accept it. These brokerage houses can be very difficult. Also, TD Ameritrade did not ask us for a copy of a revocable trust. I think, after this conversation, we should probably send it in regardless.

Howard: Yes, either that or at least a certificate of trust, which is a one or two-page summary of the relevant provisions of the trust that the financial institution needs to know in order to open an account. This way you're not walking in the same way as the power of attorney 20 years later and saying, "Hi, you don't know who I am, but I'm the trustee." They've established it at the foundation of the account. I find these national brokerage houses apply the same general financial institution policy regardless of which state they're licensed in. It's not state-specific, and they don't know the rules in that particular state regarding honoring a power of attorney.

It's important when you're dealing with a national company to make sure you get in touch with general counsel to advise them, "Florida law says X, and it's in my favor. You may not be aware of that, but now that you are, would you like to consider it before I file my papers in court, forcing you to honor my perfectly valid power of attorney?" Often, when they see the threat of litigation, and they realize that they have not been state-specific in their conduct, they will honor the power of attorney.

Julian: That's great. Is there anything we have not spoken about that you would like to share with us regarding estate planning or Medicaid planning?

Howard: One of the things I do want to touch on for sure is the importance of titling assets properly when you use a revocable trust. Many people come into my office with a trust prepared by somebody else. I'll review it and make sure it still achieves their objectives, and then I'll ask them, "Which assets are titled in your trust?" They'll look at me and say, "I don't know. I thought all of my assets were in the trust." I say, "Okay, let me take a look at your bank statements, and let's just review that together." Sure enough, in many instances, no assets have been titled in the trust. They went through the heavy lifting of creating a trust and signing it, but didn't realize you've got to retitle assets in the name of the trust in order for the assets to get into the trust.

Other times, some assets are in the trust, but some assets are not in the trust, so it's not fully funded. That's an important component of utilizing a revocable trust or any trust: You must retitle assets into the name of the trust in order for it to be effective.

HOWARD KROOKS IS A CERTIFIED ELDER LAW ATTORNEY BY THE NATIONAL ELDER LAW FOUNDATION.

Howard currently serves as chair of the Florida Bar Elder Law Section and on the board of trustees of the NAELA Foundation.

He earned his bachelor's degree in accounting from SUNY Albany and his law degree from the University of Pennsylvania Law School. Howard's practice is devoted to elder law and trust-and-estate matters. He has received many awards, including the 2006 Outstanding Achievement Award from the New York Chapter of NAELA.

Howard is a frequent lecturer and has addressed many organizations, including Barron's and Berkeley College. He has been quoted in *The Wall Street Journal* and *The New York Times* among others and has made numerous television appearances. He has written extensively on the topic of elder law. His works have been published by the New York State Bar Association.

TO CONTACT HOWARD

✉ krooks@cozen.com
🔗 https://www.cozen.com/

CHAPTER 8

ASSET PROTECTION FOR THE MIDDLE CLASS

Jason Neufeld

Julian: Your practice focuses primarily on elder law and Medicaid planning. Why don't you tell us a bit about yourself and what you do?

Jason: The firm is Elder Needs Law, and we focus on three main areas. The first is estate planning. That's your wills, your trusts, your powers of attorney. Essentially, who can make decisions for you when you're unable to make decisions for yourself and who gets your stuff after you pass away. Second is probate. For those who have not done proper planning, they sometimes have to go through the court system, and we can guide people through that process.

Third—and this is what sets us apart a bit—is something a bit more nuanced called Medicaid planning. If I could sum it up in one line, it would be asset protection for the middle class.

> If you are a multimillionaire, you can well afford to pay for your long-term care, whether it's at home or in a facility. If you're indigent, you likely already qualify for these programs that can help you. It's the working class, the middle class, who need help planning, the people who may or may not own their homes. They have maybe between $250,000 and $750,000, and they realize very quickly that long-term care at a homeowner facility is very expensive.

I legally and ethically protect my client's assets so they don't have to go broke first. They don't have to sell their house. They don't have to wait five years, and we can get them help in the near future paying for long-term care and other medical expenses.

Julian: Can you expand upon that? For example, I have a client who called me today. His wife is very ill. She either needs home care or she needs to go into a nursing home or possibly assisted living, and he's asking, "How do I get the government to pay for that so I don't have to go broke?" What's the answer?

Jason: The answer is it depends, as is often the case in the law. We have an intake form that everyone has to fill out before they talk to one of our attorneys because Medicaid in Florida treats different assets differently. They only allow you to have $2,000 in what they consider to be countable assets, but not all assets are countable. For example, IRAs, 401(k)s, and other qualified retirement plans, if they're paying out in regular distributions or required-minimum distributions, don't count as assets. That's hundreds of thousands of dollars we can take off the board in terms of figuring out how we're going to protect assets.

Money in the bank, regular stocks, bonds, anything that's non-tax-qualified is going to be an issue. If we have a spouse who themselves don't need Medicaid, it actually is a little bit easier because they're allowed to have a certain amount of assets in their name without being penalized. But when there are excess assets despite all those allowances, we have work to do. There's no one-size-fits-all option. Sometimes, it's a special-needs trust we're dealing with. Sometimes, it's something called a personal-services contract, where we're able to pay family members a lump sum for the services they're providing anyway. We have Medicaid-compliant annuities. Sometimes, there are real estate investments we're making because there are certain ways real estate can be deemed a non-accountable asset.

There are multiple options. Dring our consultation, I discuss pros and cons.

> I always tell people I don't have a magic wand solution. There's not one thing that is better than the others. But based on how your assets are allocated, we talk about potential solutions, and, based on the client's feedback, we can tailor an asset-protection plan that is going to minimize or eliminate the drawbacks and get the client access to the benefits at home or in a facility.

Julian: Let's say a husband and wife have half a million dollars, and the wife is ill. I thought you could move the money to the husband legally, and he just refuses to pay the medical bills, and that was legal.

Jason: You can do that. That's called spousal refusal. That has its own set of drawbacks as well. You really don't want to abuse that technique because when you do that, the sick spouse has to sign an assignment of support rights to the state of Florida, essentially giving Florida the ability to sue the well spouse and demand support on behalf of the sick spouse. But there are situations where that makes a lot of sense.

By the way, the state of Florida does not have a history of using that ability. But it still makes people uneasy that they even have it. We want to make sure we're doing it in a way that doesn't tempt the state to say, "This is a rich couple clearly abusing the system. We want to go after it."

Julian: I see, and the other way is you can give it away to your kids, but there's a five-year lookback period. Am I right about that?

Jason: I'm glad you brought that up because the five-year lookback period is the most misunderstood concept in my world. You cannot just give it to your kids within five years. That would be considered a gift, and if that is done within five years, it would result in a penalty depending on the size of the gift.

There are ways of getting money to the kids. For example, the personal-services contract I mentioned before would be a formal contract signed between one or more of the children and the parent seeking benefits. The idea is we have the adult children who are doing work anyway on behalf of their parents, not because they expect to get paid for work, but because that's what good sons and daughters do for their parents. They're already paying the bills. They're already driving them to the doctor. They're making sure they're their parents' advocate.

We can calculate a fair market value of that, and we will put it into a contract. Then, after the contract is signed, a lump sum of money can be transferred to one or more of the adult children. Of course, that's not without its risks or drawbacks. First of all, that payment is going to be a large lump sum, often in the six figures, that is income to the child. They're a paid caregiver. The IRS doesn't care they happen to be related to the person they're being paid to take care of. They can lose a chunk of that money to the IRS in one fell swoop.

Once it is in the child's hands, it's their money, subject to anything that's a threat to their money: divorce, death, creditors, bankruptcy, etc. In a way, it's not safe for the parent. In the right situation, that will still make sense to use as at least part of a strategy. It may, in certain situations, not make sense at all, or it may make sense to use that in conjunction with other asset-protection strategies.

Julian: I was under the impression you could move money from the ill spouse to the healthy spouse, put the ill spouse in a nursing home, and say, "She's on her own." But you're saying the state might come back and sue.

Jason: It's highly unlikely that would ever happen, but you cannot enter into the spousal-refusal strategy without signing an assignment of support rights where you give the state the ability to do that.

Julian: When you go into a nursing home, you have to go in as a paying patient, and you can do that afterwards, correct? You don't want to do that first.

Jason: It depends. Some nursing facilities will allow you to go in as what's called Medicaid-pending, where they will accept you as a resident knowing that you're applying for Medicaid, and they'll eventually get their payment. If someone goes into the facility in June, and we submitted an application, and we expect them to be approved because they're otherwise eligible, it might not get approved until July or August, but the benefits will be available in June.

If you are hospitalized, and you are discharged to a skilled nursing facility, Medicare—which everyone gets when they turn 65—will pay up to 100 days of that facility bill. It's 20 days in full. For the remaining 80 days, there might be a daily copay. It depends on your supplement or advantage plan.

That gives you many more options because every skilled nursing facility wants Medicare. They all accept Medicare. While you're on your Medicare days, we can be doing our work to protect what you have and get you eligible for Medicaid.

Julian: These facilities don't want Medicaid, right? They get paid a lot less.

Jason: It depends on the facility. The ones that are 98% full would rather have people who are privately paying, and the ones that are 70% full are going to be fine because Medicaid's just a source of money and the government pays on time. But yes,

> I think if every nursing home administrator had their way, it would be 100% privately paying patients. But that's not realistic, and every nursing facility in the state of Florida must accept Medicaid. Some people say, "Well, I don't want to

go to a nursing home that accepts Medicaid because it's a lower-level facility." I say, "They're all Medicaid nursing homes. They all accept Medicaid."

Julian: So you can go to a place like Moss getting Medicaid?

Jason: Yes. The difference is assisted-living facilities, which do not provide as high a level of care as a nursing home, have the choice. They're not required to accept Medicaid. There are plenty of fine facilities who do, but not all of them will accept Medicaid. You have to ask.

Julian: I thought Medicaid won't pay for assisted living.

Jason: It depends on the facility, and if the facility is licensed with Medicaid, depending on where you are in the state of Florida, Medicaid will pay typically between $1,500 and $1,900 per-month for the facility.

In nursing homes, your income goes to the facility, and then Medicaid pays the full difference. That's a good deal because nursing homes can cost up to $12,000 per-month. If you get Medicaid paying 10 grand a month, you're pretty happy with that.

The higher-end facilities don't accept Medicaid at all. They only accept private pay. But there are plenty of nice facilities that do. If you're in a facility that accepts $1,800 a month from Medicaid, the resident has to come up with the rest. They're partially privately paid and partially Medicaid-funded.

Julian: How did you start getting into this type of law?

Jason: I actually started out as a personal-injury lawyer. My father's a personal-injury lawyer, and I'm still affiliated with that firm, but I don't practice personal-injury law anymore. I tell you that because I wound up representing a lot of elderly people and noticed that a lot of my elderly clients who had been injured needed to be in these long-term-care facilities that are quite expensive. Even though we might have done a good job as a personal-injury lawyer getting them this big settlement, a lot of that money would eventually be lost to the facilities. I learned you could protect those assets and get Medicaid to pay for a lot of it. I said, "There's a real need for this in South Florida, and there are not a lot of attorneys doing it." It was like a revelation.

I started going to the conferences and reading the books and finding my mentors. Here I am now, 10 years later. I've found my passion. I'm serving an underserved community. A lot of people don't know what I do exists, including lawyers, which is why I love doing interviews like this. I love presenting to churches and synagogues and rotary clubs and caregiver support groups because I like to let people know that you don't have to go broke. You don't have to sell your house. You don't have to wait until you lose everything to qualify for these benefits. There are ways to get this stuff taken care of now, and it's become a real passion project of mine.

Julian: Is there any pre-planning advice you'd give to everyone, or would you say to just wait till it happens?

Jason: There are a few ways to look at that.

The first thing I tell people is that of all the fancy trusts and planning strategies I have, there's nothing more valuable than a well-drafted, durable power of attorney. A lot of people think those are one-size-fits-all documents that you can just download off the internet for free, and that's wrong. In Florida, for a power of attorney to let someone act on your behalf, it has to be very specific, meaning you can't just say, "I give my son the ability to do everything for me, so help me God." That is not allowed anymore.

These generic, boilerplate powers of attorney might be fine for doing things like banking and paying bills, but they're not good enough for me to get people access to all the planning strategies we have available.

The second thing is typically for clients who are in their mid-70s but very healthy. We can utilize what's called an irrevocable trust where we can get assets out of their names and take advantage of the fact that there's only a five-year lookback period. If we get assets out of their names, we get that clock ticking. Then, after five years, whatever's in that irrevocable trust is invisible as far as Medicaid is concerned. They can have that irrevocable trust with a financial advisor like yourself who can then work to have it grow and flourish and really be a nice-sized asset.

My sweet spot is clients who have between $100,000 and $700,000, not including their houses. That's where I'm providing the most value. When they're worth more than that, we can still help, but there's a diminishing return. It starts to make less sense because of the tax implications or the other drawbacks that go with Medicaid planning. But for the clients who have, again, $700,000, $1 million, $2 million, which is a lot of money, but not "wealthy", then utilizing that irrevocable trust can make sense. Then, when they come to me with a quarter of a million dollars, protecting that within a matter of months is very easy to do.

Julian: I think the only issue with the trust is you have to trust, no pun intended, and it's hard. You have to trust that your kids are going to take care of you. It's easier said than done.

Jason: You're absolutely right because you do lose direct control over the assets in the irrevocable trust, but you can hire and fire the trustees. Meaning if your son isn't doing what he's supposed to do, you can fire him and get someone else who's going to be thinking more about your interests. But I agree, you don't want to rely on that. You want to have the trust managed by someone you trust and whom you know has your best interests at heart, which not everybody has.

Julian: I thought in trusts you couldn't have someone that you control, such as a child or a spouse, be the trustee.

Jason: Not a spouse, but very often a child. You can also put in trust protectors. I just had a client who had around $1.5 million liquid, and we took about $1 million and put it into an irrevocable trust. They didn't have anyone they believed would do a nice job for them, so we wound up bringing in a professional fiduciary.

Julian: Are you familiar with the Wyoming cocktail?

Jason: It sounds delicious. I'm joking.

Julian: Wyoming is the only state that allows you to do a self-settled trust and remain the trustee. It's a very complicated way of doing things. You appoint a trustee in Wyoming, but you still are controlling all the assets. It seems to work, but it's very expensive. It costs around $15,000 a year to maintain. To your point, you can't do that when you have $1 million.

Given your vast amount of knowledge in your field and your years of experience, what do you wish you knew when you started that you know now?

Jason: I like to tell people that I am mostly dealing with the adult children of my actual clients. They're worried about Mom or Dad, and they have power of attorney already, and they want to help them take control. I'm always trying to tell them, sometimes unsuccessfully, that...

> long-term care is by far the biggest threat to your assets. We don't think about it while we're young. But as you get older, that will be the biggest threat to your assets.

I don't know what Medicaid's going to be like in 20 years. It may be great. They may do away with it altogether. Who the heck knows? Don't stick your head in the sand. Go get yourself long-term-care insurance or a life insurance policy with a long-term care rider or something like that. Take action now to protect yourself so you don't need Medicaid or you're less likely to need Medicaid in the future.

I say that because I'm now in my mid-40s. I waited a little bit longer than I should have to go buy long-term-care insurance. Now I have it just because of what I do. I see how important it is, and I think, "Man, I wish I'd gotten that when I was 35."

Julian: It's funny you say that because I take the other side of that argument. I just feel that it's so expensive. I have a client whose parents just turned 85. They're going to use their long-term care. But when you look at how much they have paid in over the last 40 years, they can't live long enough to get their money back.

The argument there is if you have the discipline to say, "Instead of spending this $3,000 on a premium, I'm going to put it in a separate account and not look at it." But the odds are you're not going to do that. You turn 85 and don't have the money.

Jason: I like a hybrid model of that. I agree with you; traditional long-term-care insurance is prohibitively expensive for most people. What I like are these life insurance products that have the long-term-care rider, because they're affordable. As you get older, you can access a higher percentage of the death benefit.

It has a cash-accrual component, so it's guaranteed 4% a year. You're getting better returns than that, but it's a nice, conservative CD, better than what I'm getting in my savings account. I like that there's this cash-accumulation component, and I like that no matter what, somebody's benefiting from this policy and my premiums can't go up. Either I'm going to use it when I get older, or my wife or kids are going to inherit it when I pass away because of the death benefit. No matter what, someone is going to benefit from this. But I agree with you that traditional long-term-care insurance, while probably providing a better long-term-care benefit overall, is so expensive. If you'd just invested it with Julian Rubinstein, you'd probably have more money than you know what to do with to pay for these things.

Julian: You would. But again, I'm being realistic. Let's use $5,000. If someone gave me $5,000 a year for 30 years, I would probably spend it. My friend admits that his parents would not have had it right now. They have enough to pay for 24-hour care because of their policy.

Jason: Beautiful. I love it. Right now, I would say I'm grateful that our people are getting my message, whether it's in my videos or my articles. I have a lot of speaking engagements as well. People are finding me. We're getting something like 60-to-70 calls a day, but a lot of them are people we can't help. There are people who think we're Medicaid, and they're wondering where their card is. We're being inundated with calls we can't serve. We have to sift through all these messages and find the people who really do need our help. We try to get back to everybody. Even if we can't help them, we want to get them to the right resource where they can get the help they need. We give out a ton of free information all the time, and we're happy to do it. It is a challenge, but it's good challenge to have.

JASON NEUFELD IS THE MANAGING PARTNER OF ELDER NEEDS LAW, PPLC.

 Jason is an "AV" preeminent-rated attorney by Martindale-Hubbell, and is consistently recognized as a top lawyer among his peers in Super Lawyers Magazine and Florida Trends Legal Elite (2012- 2023).

Jason specializes in elder needs law with focuses in Medicaid planning, estate planning, and probate administration. He is on the board of the Academy of Florida Elder Law Attorneys and Co-Chair of the Broward County Bar Association Elder Law Section. Jason teaches other elder law attorneys about Medicaid planning and regularly presents in front of community organizations.

Jason wrote the book *How to Get Medicaid to Pay for Some or All of Your Long-Term Care Expenses: Without Having to Wait Five Years, Without Having to Sell Your House, and Without Having to Go Broke First.*

TO CONTACT JASON

✉ jason@elderneedslaw.com
🔗 https://www.elderneedslaw.com/
https://www.elderneedsinsurance.com/

CHAPTER 9

OWN NOTHING, CONTROL EVERYTHING

Hillel Pressser

Julian: As a lawyer, you specialize in asset protection. You've also published two books. With that said, why don't you tell us a bit about yourself and your law firm?

Hillel: We specialize in asset protection, and we have a nationwide practice based in Boca Raton, Florida. We have clients all over the country and in different countries as well, and we specialize both in domestic and foreign asset protection. People work very hard for what they have. It's not my job to make them richer. I want to make sure they don't become one penny poorer.

Julian: I like that. You earn it and keep it. But Florida is a very litigious state. People like to sue for everything, I'm told. We have some of the highest property claims in the country, at least that's what my condo board tells us. What are some of the strategies you tell people to employ?

Hillel: There are so many different strategies, and we don't believe in doing any cookie-cutter work. We take a very comprehensive approach to planning. I want to make sure that everyone's plan is individualized and customized and tailored to their personal and their business needs. Someone may be protecting against a teenager driving their car, others against a third marriage, and you're going to do those in different ways. All in all, we always want to tell our clients to essentially own nothing but control everything. If you own something, it's yours to lose. I don't want to own anything. I don't want to lose it. I worked hard. I don't want to start all over.

Julian: That sounds perfect, but how do you accomplish that?

Hillel:

> One of the most common strategies is transferring assets into protective entities. To oversimplify it, say you have a vacation home in your name, and you get sued; you can lose that vacation home. If you have a rental property in your name, and somebody gets injured on the rental property, they can sue you because you own that rental property. But if, instead, you take that asset, and you transfer it out of your name into a protective entity, it's no longer yours to lose.

There are so many different types of protective entities. There are LLCs, limited partnerships, corporations, trusts, etc. Again, there's no one size that fits all. But it's really the coolest thing in the world, because just like you and I are different people, you and your protective entity are different living individuals. You have a social security number; your protective entity has a tax ID number, so the law looks at you as two totally separate people. I love protective entities. They're among my favorite strategies.

Julian: When you transfer something to an LLC, how do you still control it? I thought if you control the LLC, it's considered part of your property

Hillel: Not at all. Depending on what state you're in, things are different. But if we're talking Florida, you'll have what's called a manager-managed LLC. That means anybody can own the LLC. I can own the LLC. You can own the LLC. Another company can own the LLC. However, if I'm the manager, I'm the one who controls it. Take that piece of property out of your name so you don't own it, put it in the LLC, or whatever the protective entity is. I'm just using the LLC as an example, but if you're the manager of the LLC, you control it as if you owned it without the actual ownership.

> The goal with asset protection is essentially to take your chips off the table. You want to make it so difficult and expensive for anybody to collect against you that they don't want to sue you in the first place. You don't want to be the low-hanging fruit.

If they do sue you, you want to be able to settle the case for 5, 10, 15 cents on the dollar. The whole point of asset protection is to make yourself uncollectible and judgment-proof, and that way you're not a good candidate to be sued. Nobody wants to sue you if they can't collect against you.

Julian: I guess the same holds true for your liquid investments or stocks and bonds.

Hillel: Absolutely. It doesn't matter what the asset is; if those liquid assets are in your name, you can lose them. But again, if you take them out of your name, and you put them into some sort of protective entity, no one can touch them. You might take your liquid assets and put them in a trust. You may put them in a limited partnership. You may put them in an LLC. Again, there's no one size that fits all, but the main goal is to get them out of your name and into some sort of protective entity where no one can touch them. What that protective entity is just depends on the person.

Julian: Interesting. Just to digress a little, what made you get into this type of law?

Hillel: If you'd asked me when I was 10 years old what I was going to be, I would've told you hands-down I was going to be a lawyer. With that being said, I've always loved business. Asset protection is really the perfect marriage of business and law. Most of my clients are business owners.

I met a mentor a very long time ago. He was one of the grandfathers of asset protection, and he had done asset protection for people in my family. He said he wouldn't hire me. He said I couldn't work for free, not that I wasn't good, but he just didn't need anyone. I said, "Okay, no problem. I'll hire you." I became his client, and he ended up being a mentor to me and a partner of mine. Unfortunately, he passed away about 13 years ago.

Julian: You actually never worked for a firm, then. You came out of law school and started your own firm?

Hillel: Not exactly. When I first got out of law school, I was a prosecutor, and I did that for a year or two because I wanted to have the ability to try cases. When you're a prosecutor, you walk in the first day, and they hand you a box of 200 cases and tell you, "You have 40 trials coming up." I wanted to get that litigation experience. I wanted to get that trial experience. After that, I moved into asset protection.

But I had actually been studying asset protection before that, even in law school, reading every book and article I could, meeting everyone in the industry I could. I just wanted to get that experience.

Julian: What do you wish you knew when you started that you know now?

Hillel: Everything. You can't buy experience. If I knew then what I know now, I'd be like a superhero.

Julian: What is one thing you share with almost every client? I probably know the answer: Own nothing and control everything.

Hillel: Of course. But really the most important thing is to educate yourself. People don't wake up in the morning and expect to be sued, but there are so many lawsuits. The last time I checked, it was something like a hundred million lawsuits every single year. There was about a one-in-four chance you'd be sued in the next 12 months, and the average person and business is sued about five times over their lifetime.

The stat that gets me the most is that you're seven times more likely to face a lawsuit than to get in a car accident. Everybody has car insurance. The first thing I tell people is to educate yourself and know that there are options. Just this morning, I had a client call me and refer me to another client. I would have loved to have been able to help him, but unfortunately, he called me way too late. The lawsuit is over, judgments are there, and there's nothing I can do. The biggest thing to understand is that there are things you can do there to protect your wealth, but you have to be proactive.

Julian: What would you say is your unique approach to your clients that separates you from other asset-protection lawyers?

Hillel: First of all, asset protection is a niche. There might be a hundred estate-planning attorneys in every city or a hundred personal-injury attorneys in every city. There are probably only a few hundred people in the country that claim they do asset protection. Of those few hundred, five or six firms get 80% of the business. Why I think people come to us and what sets us apart is we take a more holistic approach.

People come to us from all across the country for asset protection, but we also have estate-planning attorneys. We have tax specialists. We have business-succession-planning specialists. Although we're always looking at asset protection first and foremost, I'm also looking at the integrated approach. I'm looking at things from an asset-protection point of view, an estate-planning point of view, a tax-planning point of view, a business-succession planning point of view, a financial-planning point of view, and an accounting point of view.

The point is, while you're alive, you want to take your chips off the table. You want to make sure you're uncollectible and judgment-proof, but when you pass away, you also want to make sure that those assets go where you want them to go. You can't just have asset protection alone on an island.

I think a lot of people come to us for our credibility and our knowledge. I've written several books on asset protection. There was a time I was giving 50-100 paid speeches all across the country on asset protection every year. We helped to rewrite some of the asset-protection laws. I've taught law, so no lack of knowledge there.

Julian: You said something very interesting, which I want to point out. It's also a great tool for inheritance. If you're over the limit, start trying to save on estate taxes using some of your structures. Am I correct?

Hillel: Yes, and you bring up two points. You talk about inheritance and you talk about estate tax, and to me they're different things. Someone will come in here with a great estate plan, like a will and a trust, which may say, "When John Smith is 30, he gets a third. When he's 40, he gets a third." What if when John Smith is 30, he's going through a divorce? You just lost half of that third. What if at age 40, John Smith's being sued for a car accident? You just lost half of that third.

When it comes to inheritance, you need to make sure you have all the asset-protection clauses built into the estate planning. You can fix that with a few words. Maybe, instead of when John Smith is 30, he gets a third, when John Smith is 30, the trustee shall consider giving him a third. Those two words, shall consider, take it from an estate plan with no asset protection to an estate plan with asset protection. That can literally save everything.

In regards to the estate taxes, absolutely. Everyone pays a lot of taxes when they're alive and making money. People try their best, legally and ethically, to pay as little as possible when they pass away. There are a lot of things you can do where asset protection is integrated with the estate plan and the tax plan. You can get assets out of your name for estate-tax purposes. That way, you don't have to answer to your kids for a slice of pizza because you've given them everything while you're alive.

Julian: You're saying that you take the money out of your estate, but you maintain control, so you can use it for income if you need it. You don't have to go to your kids and beg and borrow.

Hillel: It's not even necessarily that you can use it for income, but there are very specific ways. One example is a limited partnership. The limited partnership may have a general partner that controls the limited partnership. The limited partnership then may be filled with assets. Someone then may gift the ownership interest they own in the limited partnership to the trust for their kids, so it's outside of their estate. But as long as they retain that general-partnership interest, they still have control over the limited partnership and thus have control over the assets of the limited partnership. Again, there's no one size that fits all, and you probably need a lot more time to explain it, but there are definitely things you can do from an estate-tax position as well.

Julian: In Florida, we tell everyone to start with joint tenants in the entirety to make it simple. That's probably the first thing to do, correct?

Hillel: Yes. Tenancy by entirety exists in about 25 different states. As you mentioned, Florida is one of them. They're only for a married, living couple.

If there's a divorce, you can't have it. If there's a death, you can't have it. But if you are married and living, it's a great thing to have. It doesn't cost you a penny. Essentially, what tenancy by entirety states is that the assets of both spouses are not subject to the creditors of one spouse.

A good example is if a husband has $100,000 in his account, and a wife has $100,000 in her account, if the husband gets sued, he loses the $100,000. If the wife gets sued, she loses the $100,000. If the husband and wife instead take their money and put it in a joint account, and it's labeled by tenancy by entirety, now, if the husband gets sued, they can't take anything. Now, if the wife gets sued, they can't take anything. They can only go after those assets if both the husband and wife are sued, which normally doesn't happen. Normally, one is sued in business, another is sued for a car accident, and things of that nature. My wife tells me I only married her to get the tenancy by entirety protection, and she may be accurate. I joke of course.

Julian: I heard you have to be careful with your car insurance with tenancy by entirety if you own the car yourself.

Hillel: Cars are really important, and it's not really the insurance so much as it is the titling.

Obviously, the biggest lawsuits you see are car accidents. They're really easy to get away from, and here's how. If you have a car, it should only be titled to the primary driver. If a husband has a car that he drives 80% of the time, it should be in his name and his name alone. If the wife has a car that she drives 80% of the time, it should be in her name and her name alone. The reason for that is, if there's ever a car accident, both the driver and the owner are sued.

For example, if you have a car that's titled to the husband, but the wife or the kid is driving it, if the wife or kid get in a car accident, they get sued as the driver, and the husband gets sued as the owner. The best way to avoid the car-accident lawsuits is to only title the car to one person, and the one person should be who drives the car the majority of the time.

Julian: How do you deal with that? If the wife is not working, can she still lease? Will she have enough credit to lease the car because she's married?

Hillel: Yes, presumably that's going to be fine. Worst case, if you had to sign as a guarantor on the loan, you could. The key thing is to make sure you're not on the title.

Take that a step further. You don't want your car titled to your business. Now, let me preface it. I'm not talking about fleets of vehicles. If you're a builder, and you have 50 cars, that's a different story.

But you don't want your personal vehicle titled to your business, because if you go out for dinner on Saturday night and you get in an accident, now your entire business is sued and put at risk because it is the owner of the vehicle.

I see so many business owners who title their cars to their businesses because they want the expense. But just because it's titled to you and not your business doesn't mean you can't take the expense. It's still reasonable, depending on how much you use it for business, but you don't ever want your primary vehicle titled to your business.

Julian: That's very good advice. Let me ask, with all the success you have, what is your biggest challenge?

Hillel: My biggest challenge is probably just growing. One of our goals and missions is to passionately educate all generations on wealth protection and asset protection. As a business owner, the toughest thing for me has always been finding and hiring good people. I live in South Florida, and a lot of people choose to come down here, not because they want to work 20 hours a day, but because they want to enjoy the outside, and they want to walk and bike and go to the beach, which I totally understand and respect. I'm a big proponent of work-life balance. But I always say, "If I can hire endless great people, we would grow much more and help a lot more people."

HILLEL L. PRESSER, Esq., MBA IS THE MANAGING PARTNER AT THE PRESSER LAW FIRM, P.A. SPECIALIZING IN ASSET PROTECTION.

Hillel represents individuals and businesses in connection with the establishment of comprehensive asset-protection plans that incorporate both domestic and international components.

Hillel graduated from the School of Management at Syracuse University, where he was one of the first students to major in entrepreneurship. He then obtained his law degree from Nova Southeastern University and later completed his Masters in Marketing at Lynn University. He also served as an Adjunct Faculty Member (Law) at Lynn University.

Hillel Presser has been featured in numerous newspapers and magazines and has authored several books and articles on asset protection and law, as well as helping to rewrite several asset-protection laws. He has engaged in hundreds of presentations throughout the country.

TO CONTACT HILLEL

✉ hp@assetprotectionattorneys.com
🔗 https://www.assetprotectionattorneys.com/

CHAPTER 10

FAMILY INCLUSION IN WEALTH PLANNING & MANAGEMENT

Evan W. Turk

Julian: You're the founding member of the law firm, E.W. Turk, and Of-Counsel for The Ticktin Law Group. Why don't you tell us a little bit about yourself and your practice?

Evan: My background is in finance. I practice law in what I call wealth management, which incorporates my background in understanding financial strategies.

> What I do for my clients is I look at their whole picture and try to diagnose where their vulnerabilities are, whether it's creditor issues or family structures. I try to reduce their liability. The lowest hanging fruit is their tax implications.

I try to work with all of their professionals, whether it's their CPA or their financial advisor, and create a concise plan that is not only actionable but understandable. I try to decipher what is noise versus what is actionable and try to help our clients pragmatically in a way that makes sense for them and their families.

Julian: When did you start your practice? When did you go out on your own?

Evan: Before I was a lawyer, I was in finance. I was a Series 7 financial advisor. I had my own financial company during law school. I went to law school at night, and I was principal of my own financial company. Upon graduation, I sold it. I worked for a year in advanced insurance strategies with the uber wealthy, and I decided to go out on my own. I'm admitted to practice in front of the United States Tax Court. I'm also admitted to practice within the states of Florida and New Jersey. I have been doing this since about 2008.

Julian: You joined just as the great financial crisis started.

Evan: I got to be a part of it. It's almost as if some people knew it was going to happen before it happened.

Julian: When people got nervous this year with the stock market and inflation, I said, "If we can live through '08, we can live through anything." It was so funny how people said, "No, this time is different." I said, "No, this time is inflation. That time the entire financial system was about to crumble. This is just noise."

Evan: Exactly. It's stressful because when you're looking at your financial statements, it's an emotional piece. You don't get your real estate value every month, but you get your financial value every month. You look at it from a different perspective because it's in front of you, whereas other assets are not, especially when you own real estate.

Julian: You don't look at your house value, yet when you go to sell, it's most always higher than when you paid for it. It's the same thing with a stock. If you hold onto it long enough, it always goes up in value. You just have to be patient.

What's the most important thing you share with your clients? Is there one go-to piece of advice you always give them?

Evan: One of the things I really need to understand is what their family structure is. Most people try to protect their wealth, but they don't realize their biggest vulnerabilities lie within their own family structure, whether it's divorce or children that may have some issues or concerns.

> Understanding family is the most valuable piece of information I can gather from my clients. It is the foundation of what we do in our plans. Whether my clients have families with grandchildren, great-grandchildren, or no children whatsoever, the foundation lies in where they're going with their families involved. It's the biggest asset they have. It's also the biggest liability.

Julian: What would you say is the biggest mistake many people make?

Evan: Marriage. But, all jokes aside, when you do asset protection, a lot of people put assets into their names jointly with their spouses, and then their spouses end up filing for divorce. All of a sudden, a big percentage of one's wealth is now gone because they showed to the courts that they meant those assets to be joint assets. Once they become joint assets, they're hard to unwind, so a lot of clients who are seeking asset protection are actually making themselves more vulnerable. That's the biggest mistake.

The other one is just setting up assets individually in your name rather than using an asset-protection trust or a limited-liability company structure. You're becoming vulnerable in a world that's highly litigious. When you have an economy that is potentially going towards a recession, lawsuits happen exponentially. Looking at how your assets are titled and who they're titled with is by far the most important thing I do.

Julian: Let's start with someone who's on a second marriage. They already have some assets put away. You're saying a mistake is they get married a second time and immediately make all these assets joint and get themselves in trouble?

Evan: The first mistake they make is they enter marriage without a prenuptial agreement.

> If done correctly, a prenuptial agreement is there to protect both parties. Even so, about 90% of people enter marriage without a prenuptial.

The next thing that they do is that out of love and for all the right reasons emotionally, they share their wealth with their significant others. They open joint bank accounts, they add their names to other assets, and they do this out of love. Unfortunately, things change. People get divorced. Especially if somebody's been divorced once, the chance of them getting divorced a second time is exponentially higher.

It's not the most romantic thing to do: planning against the person you love the most, but it's the most essential, because more likely than not, if there's a problem, that's where it's going to stem from.

Julian: Are prenups being upheld in the state of Florida right now?

Evan: Absolutely, as long as you have fair disclosure, and you're doing it without undue influence. In other words, as long as both parties are entering it knowing what they're entering into, it'll be upheld. It becomes problematic when, a day before your wedding, you sign into a prenuptial agreement because you're told that if you don't sign this prenup, we're not getting married tomorrow. Those are the ones that become problematic.

But I'm also doing a lot of postnuptial agreements, people who want to stay together, but if they don't, they don't want to go through the nightmare of having to deal with litigation and divorce. It's still one of the worst things you can go through, a lawsuit with somebody you loved. Sometimes people still love their spouses, and they're going through divorce against their wishes. Now they're not only losing their significant other, but they're losing at least half of their assets.

Julian: Having gone through divorce, I think a postnuptial when things are getting rocky probably is good because cooler heads will prevail and less emotions are in the room. Both sides get a better outcome.

Evan: It lessens the risk and the anxiety associated with a failing relationship, because if you don't have it, you are now entering a world of litigation, and the only ones who really profit from this are the attorneys.

One thing I do not understand is there are family law attorneys that love to instigate. They love to tell their clients that they're entitled to more: Let's fight, fight, fight. At the end of the day, the only one who's winning is the attorney.

Julian: I agree with you. In fact, having gone through a prenup, it's amazing how even when both parties agree, the lawyers try to cause trouble to create more work. It's really a shame. You're absolutely right.

Evan: It's sad. The law has made big strides in the realm of collaborative divorce. It's a great idea. But in reality, very few people are taking advantage of it. The attorneys really don't want to be in that space because they're going to lose a gigantic revenue model for themselves.

Julian: Putting asset protection aside for the moment, if someone sets up just a Florida LLC, does that help them in divorce at all to shield their assets?

Evan: It depends. That's your typical lawyer answer. It can help if it's set up correctly.

Julian: For younger people first starting out in asset protection, is there anything they can do other than a prenup?

Evan: Setting up an LLC structure, not co-mingling assets, having a good accountant and a bookkeeper, and making sure that money is accounted for are all things they can do to mitigate risk. Often, people take money outside of their

LLC structure and put it into their own personal accounts. They don't account for it as a loan, or they don't write off their taxes properly, and they're not using the fullest extent of the law and what they're entitled to. A lot of our clients have cars that are written off on the business, but it has to be done correctly. If it's not, it becomes a marital asset.

Julian: I thought that for someone who's working, all the income is marital, that you can't segregate it.

Evan: It depends on what your income is. If you have an LLC or a partnership or a corporation, sometimes it may make sense to have a C-corporation to separate business assets, business income, retained earnings versus personal income.

People don't realize when they fill out mortgage applications or credit card applications that they're making a public record of their income that could be used against them later. Especially for entrepreneurs, that becomes a big risk.

Julian: Interesting. What would you say is your unique approach with your clients that sets you apart from other firms in this space?

Evan: My background is in finance first, so one of the things I realized is that a lot of the tax-mitigation strategies can be derived from the financial plan and understanding the financial strategy.

A lot of my peers like to set up a trust, whether it's revocable or irrevocable, and they can generate large legal fees and make you look very sophisticated. But at the end of the day, if you work with the financial advisor, understand the underlying financial strategy, trusts and fancy trusts become more problematic than beneficial.

Julian: What do you wish you knew when you started that you know now?

Evan: I think when you're younger as an attorney, you want to prove how smart you are and you create the most incredible legal documents, but nobody understands them. The best analogy I can give you right now is to think about buying a car 10 years ago. You wouldn't need a lesson on how to use the car. There was no computer system. If you wanted to put the air conditioning on, you pressed the button that said AC. Nowadays, the cars are so sophisticated that just to get the heated seats on, you have to select options on the computer panel.

Sometimes as we get more sophisticated, we forget that saying, "Keep it simple stupid." I've learned the best strategy is the one your clients understand rather than having them have to trust that you know what you're doing. Most of the time the mistake is not in the plan; it's the implementation of the plan.

Julian: I think people like you and I forget that people don't understand what we're saying sometimes. We take it for granted. With interest rates finally rising, we now buy money markets, but most of my younger clients have no idea what that is. They don't even know what interest income is, and it's not their fault because for the last 20 years, you didn't earn interest. I've had to educate them all on why we're using a money market and how it has no risks.

Evan: It's funny because the older generation thought of CDs as compact discs, and now the new generation has never heard of them as compact discs or certificates of deposit. They'll say, "What is this? You mean the bank will give you a higher interest rate and it's insured?"

Julian: Is there anything else you'd like to discuss that we haven't covered?

Evan: It's important to understand that sound planning is not a process where you need to sell the client a specific trust or overall investment. It's about taking the time to understand who your clients are and how you can be of value. What sets us apart is we really are bespoke to understanding exactly what our clients' needs are and including the family as much as possible, because there are tremendous tax benefits if you include the family. You also encourage the family to do the right thing.

When you include a strategy that incorporates the family, now the family is working for a purpose rather than entitled to receive. My favorite thing to do is to increase everyone's happiness by encouraging families to work together as a business rather than as an entitlement structure where the children think they're entitled because from day one the parents are just giving them stuff.

I have an eleven-year-old and a nine-year-old. I try to have them work with me to get a better understanding of the family structure, because they're not learning this in school. If you want an entrepreneurial spirit, you have to teach them young rather than assuming they're going to figure this out when they're older.

That's the one bit of advice I tell everybody: Include your family so you're teaching them how to fish instead of giving them fish.

EVAN W. TURK, Esq., IS AN ATTORNEY AND ENTREPRENEUR AND IS OF-COUNSEL WITH THE TICKTIN LAW GROUP.

Evan advises successful entrepreneurs, family offices, and affluent families on ways to reduce their tax liability while protecting and growing their wealth.

Evan is the author of *Asset Protection by Design*. His career started on Wall Street and is focused on his experience in finance, tax and the law. He is licensed to practice law in Florida and New Jersey and is duly qualified and admitted to practice before the United States Tax Court.

TO CONTACT EVAN

✉ ewt@ewturklaw.com
🔗 https://www.ewturk.com/

Part 4

BUSINESS
FINANCES

CHAPTER 11

THE MINDSET OF AN ENTREPRENEUR

Bill Forster

Julian: You've had businesses in several industries. You've also written a book. Why don't you tell us how you got started?

Bill: I have been an entrepreneur since I was in my 20s. I'm now 78, so I've got many years of storytelling and experiences. My kids always liked to hear the stories. One afternoon, my grandson said, "Why don't you write a book about all these stories? They're great." I'd never written a book in my life, but it wasn't the first time I tried to do something I'd never done.

I wrote a book about my experiences as an entrepreneur, entitled *If It Weren't For My Wife, I'd Be Living In A Trailer*. It takes a strong wife to put up with an entrepreneur, particularly if you have your ups and downs as everybody does. During the good times, things are great. During the bad times, they're absolutely horrible. Sometimes you make a lot of money, and sometimes you lose all your money. She's been stuck with me for all these years, and we had just celebrated our 50-something anniversary, so I named it after her.

The book tells the stories of my life the way I wrote it. It wasn't well-written. It's just something I did and sent to Amazon, and they printed it. I thought it was just going to be for my family and friends. I never thought I had the talent to write a book, but I discovered a hidden talent. I've written a couple of books since then. As an entrepreneur, I wasn't afraid to go one step further, and I did. That's how the book got started.

Julian: I know you've had some great business success in various countries, including some ventures in Russia and South Africa.

Bill: I've been to 30 countries in my years of work. South Africa was the one I went to the most, but I did go to Russia as well.

Julian: Tell us a little bit about Russia, considering all that's going on in the world today.

Bill: I was already in the import business when Russia came about. It was before 1984. A friend of mine said, "Why don't you ever go to Russia?" I said, "I'm happy to go to Russia, but I don't know anything about it." At that time, the Jewish Federations were bringing in all the Russians. I think it was called Mission Abraham. There was a Russian guy who came to Norfolk, where I lived. I met him and asked him what he could do for me. He said he had good connections in Russia, and that he could get almost anything I needed. So we got our visas and got ready to go to Russia.

I had a big business at that time with Best Products catalog store. People don't probably know who they are today, but Best Products had a big section in office furniture. I tried to do some of the sourcing for that when I was in Taiwan and other places, so I knew something about it. I called the head buyer of that department and asked him how big the category was, and he told me it was gigantic. I said, "What margins are you generally working on?" He told me his margins. I grabbed the Best Products catalog and went to Russia. I didn't know much about knockdown furniture other than that was what I bought for my offices.

The Russian guy took me to a factory outside of Kiev. It wasn't just a factory; it was a complex. They had a big building where they must have had 100 or more draftsman and engineers drawing up furniture. I gave the guy we met at the factory a copy of the Best Products book, and they took me to their showroom, which was mammoth, maybe a third the size of a K-Mart. All kinds of furniture all over the place. We looked at the book, and he pointed out different items in the room, saying, "This is yours, this is yours, this is yours." Everything in that book they had done. The difference was they did it in solid wood. Best Products was buying it in laminated wood. As anybody knows, there's a big difference in value between laminated wood and solid wood.

They took the book. They called a meeting in their conference room. 20 guys on their side showed up with notepads, and then in came this older gentleman who reminded me of my grandfather. He was the chairman. We started going through the book, and they gave me a price. I had set my goal on the Best Products retail at less than 50%, which was way beyond even for laminated, and that was the price I targeted. That would give me good margins to bring it in. Well, they started to give me a hard time on my prices. It's too high. We were going back and forth, like any negotiation.

Time for lunch. The chairman tells me to come with him. I went to shake his hand, and I noticed he had a rash on his hands. I used to have those rashes, and I had the cream in my briefcase because I never knew when they would come. I said to him, "Let me put this cream on your hands. Make you feel good." By the time he got to his office, he was feeling great. The rash had gone. We sat down. We had every flavored shot of vodka one could imagine. I'm not a big drinker, so I was careful, but he was downing them one at a time. I told him he reminded me of my grandfather, and we talked about where he was born.

He said, "Can you really bring us this business?" I said, "Yes, I can bring you millions of dollars of this business, but I need to have a price that works for my buyer." I gave a price which I thought was fair and that my buyer would accept, and that hopefully he would make money, and we would make a very nice income from it after paying the freight and bringing it in. We went back to the conference room. He sat down, and in front of his 20 people, he said, "We're going to start over. Bill is my grandson, and anything he wants, you give him." All I wanted was the 50% off, and that was what I got. On every item, they gave me 50% off.

Then, he was called into an office for an emergency call. He came back out, white as a ghost. He told me he had just gotten a call from the Kremlin, and they were decentralizing businesses, so he was now the owner of this furniture complex, which consisted of 400 factories all over Russia. He says, "You're my hero. We're going to take every order you give us, and we're going to ship it." I was as happy as a dog in the woods.

We left there and went right to the port. We had to go up three flights of stairs to get to the chief of the port. This big guy with rosy cheeks, his uniform busting at the buttons, was behind the desk. I was really cocky. I knew I had a good program here, and I've had plenty of experience importing. I knew I should be able to get a contract rate for my volume. The guy says, "What can I do for you?" I said, "It's very simple. I need to book 1,000 containers." He said, "1,000?"

Then he laughed as hard as he could. His face got red, and tears started coming down his cheeks. He kept smacking his desk. We didn't know what was going on. We sat there for five minutes while this guy was having the best time of his life. He finally called me over to the window overlooking the port. He said, "You see that ship over there?" I said, "Yeah." He says, "What do you see?" I said, "I see a little ship. A little cargo ship with containers on top of the deck." He said, "Those are our ships. They are all like that. There are no containers under the deck like you're used to. They're all on top of the deck. Maybe we get 100 containers on every ship, but all of them are already consigned to Smirnoff. I have no ship for you and no containers. Even if I did, my containers are not approved by the universal exchange of containers. We ship them, they unload them, and they send them back. Even if I were to have a ship and were to have transferable containers, I've got another problem."

I said, "What's that?"

He said, "Your factory is 500 miles away, and the roads are horrible. Also, we don't have that many trucks. If we did have that many trucks, we don't have the containers to put on the trucks. But even if we did, we would send the trucks, and they would break down. No question about it. It would take us three months to find out where they were and to fix them. We could use trains, maybe. But how do I unload the rail cars here at the port? I don't have that kind of equipment."

Basically, that was the end of the program. I looked at my guys and said, "Okay, let's go home. All this was for nothing." We did. That was my experience in Russia.

Julian: That's a very interesting experience.

Bill: Every country I went to was an interesting experience. For instance, I was at the hardware show in Virginia, and this big, tall Afrikaans kid, about 23 years old, came into my booth. He said, "I'd like to show you my gazebos. My dad and I make gazebos in South Africa." I said, "Okay." He showed me the gazebos. I said, "Johann, I can't sell those. It's not my line of business. But maybe I can find someone who can. Why don't you stand in my booth, and as customers come by, I'll introduce you to them."

We did that. Eventually, my friend, the merchandise manager of Fortunoff, came to the booth. I said to him, "Meet Johann." They talked, and when my friend left, Johann came to me and said, "I just got an order for $250,000. What commission do you want?" I said to him, "When I told you to come in my booth, I told you I didn't want a commission. Nothing's changed. I still don't want a commission. I'm glad you got the order. That's great."

He said, "Well, it's a big decision for us. It's a big order. I'll have my father fly over right away." The father flew over. Two days later, we were sitting in my booth, and the father says, "I can't believe what you did for my son. We have to pay you a commission." I said, "Again, I don't want a commission. I'm happy to do it for you."

The father left the kid sitting in my booth, and he was looking at my wire-stacking chair. If you know what they are, these would be the wire grid chairs in front of Home Depot and everything that sold at that time for $9.99. He said, "Where do you get those from?" I said, "I get them from China or Taiwan." He said, "Well, can you give me the specifications?" I said, "Sure, I'll give them to you." I gave him the specifications. He took pictures, and the show was over.

About four months later, I got a phone call from this kid. He said, "I have your chair. I have a manufacturer that can make your chair around the price you want it." I said, "Well, that's amazing. Can you tell me anything about the factories?" He said, "It is a big factory. They make outdoor furniture. Come to South Africa."

I got my visa, and I made my reservation to go to South Africa. My wife was going crazy: "Why are you doing this? It's dangerous."

But I went anyway. We got to Johannesburg in the dead of night, and it was the first time I saw one of those V-shaped bottom Jeeps carrying guys with automatic machine guns. I said, "Holy crap, this is it." We went in, got our luggage, and I got in a cab. I said to the cab driver, "I want to go to the hotel in Johannesburg." He said, "Okay." We drove in pitch darkness. It took an hour, but we started to see some lights. I said, "Is that Johannesburg?" He said, "No, that's Soweto." I said, "What is Soweto?" He said, "That's where my people live. You go into Johannesburg." I said, "Okay."

We got to the hotel. It was beautiful. I asked the receptionist, "Where's the biggest synagogue in Johannesburg?" They told me it was the Great Synagogue. I went there first thing in the morning for Dominion.

I went back to my hotel where Johann was going to pick me up. He picked me up with his agent, a banker. They took me to a factory in Johannesburg. I walk in. There's a mezuzah on the door. The two owners were wearing yarmulkes. I said, "I'm home. This is going to be pretty damn good." They said, "We've opened up a place in Bophuthatswana." That's one of the homeland developments that the South Africans built for the Black communities. He said, "We have a factory in Bophuthatswana. We are now making that chair. We will show you."

We went to the factory in Bophuthatswana. A stately Black man is sitting behind his desk, and behind him is this white South African. They asked me, "What are you here for?" I said, "I'm here to buy these steel chairs." They said, "Okay. How many are you going to buy?" I told them. They said, "All right, let's see what we can do."

Their prices were nowhere near what I needed. They didn't understand it, and they told us that the problem was steel was too high. Iscor, the steel producer in South Africa, controlled the price of steel domestically. Although they were cheapest in the world, domestic buyers couldn't get that price.

We left there, went right to Iscor, and talked to the export manager. We told them we wanted to buy all these chairs, put 1,000 people to work, and we needed this factory to get those steel prices. They granted it. Now they had no problem meeting my prices, and that year we were the largest shipper of containers out of South Africa. Johann the banker, who became my agent at that point, was on the front page of the South African Johannesburg paper: "Number one exporter in the country." How many clients did he have? One. Me. How much business did he have? Mine. But he was the exporter of the year. That was how I did business in South Africa.

Julian: How long did it last?

Bill: That business lasted one whole year. We sold over a million chairs. I made 50 cents a chair instead of the 10 cents I was making out of China, and I was doing great. I went back to South Africa. I designed a chair in all PVC with colored handles. I went to Swaziland and bought a wood picnic set, so now I'm going to import three items. I'm going to go crazy.

I came home and needed a sales manager. I had too much to do. I called Bob Kresky, the son-in-law to the owner, and asked, "Bob, who's the best sales manager in the country for outdoor furniture?" He said, "Don Corning." I called Don and told him, "I want to offer you a job." He said, "I don't want a job. I'm happy." I said, "Don, I'll double your salary." He said, "Well, maybe I can meet you for breakfast."

We met and I told him the story. It didn't matter what his salary was. I didn't care if he told me $300,000. I needed him. He was the best, and I had plenty of money. He said, "Look, I think what you did is terrific, but I'm with the biggest outdoor furniture company in the country. I love my boss. I like my position. Why don't we take over your marketing, and you just do the logistics of importing? You've got to meet my president."

We went to the factory. We met the president, Ray. I told him what we were doing and what I was able to buy going into the next year. He said, "Would you be interested in a joint venture?" I said, "Sure." He said, "How much business do you think you're going to write on these items?" I said, "$20 million." He looked at Don and said, "Do you think that's possible?" Don said, "Absolutely. The chairs alone are going to be $15 million." Ray said, "Okay, we're owned by the Sunbeam Corporation, and I'm going to get permission to do a joint venture with you. Once I get it, we'll get the lawyers to draw up an agreement."

I went home, and he called me back a week later. He said, "We're going to do it. $20 million, and you're going to make 20% of our profits." I said, "Okay." I was going to make a couple million dollars. The lawyers sent the agreements. I sent them to my lawyer. They went back and forth. Finally, I had a good agreement, and I was going to sign it on Monday morning.

That Sunday, the Sunday Times had a big front page story about riots in South Africa, with a picture of a white man beating a Black man with a whip. I said, "Oh, this is not going to be good." That morning, I got a call from the NAACP, who would've been at Bosco's and saw one of my chairs, and it was labeled Bophuthatswana. But I put in an apostrophe so it read like Botswana. He said, "Mr. Forster, was your chair made in Bophuthatswana or Botswana?" I said, "Bophuthatswana." He said, "Tomorrow morning, we are going to riot in front of Bosco's, and it'll be covered in all the papers, and you're going to have to stop importing these chairs."

I called Ray and said, "I'm not going to sign the agreement. This is what just happened, and I'm not going to put you in jeopardy in my place. It's like transferring a disease, so I can't do the contract. I'm out of business. I can't import from South Africa anymore." Not long afterward, the Commerce Department put an embargo on South Africa. I was definitely out of business.

Ray invited me to the factory again and said, "You and I haven't known each other a long time, but I'm just amazed at what you're able to do, and I know you have a great history in Taiwan. I also buy from Taiwan." I said, "What do you buy?" He said, "I buy umbrellas, chairs, tables, you name it. I've got a $10-million import program. Do you think you can get better prices than me?" I said, "No doubt." I'm cocky. I'm a good negotiator. I learned how to negotiate in Taiwan, and no price is ever their lowest price. We made a deal. He said, "I'll pay you 10% of whatever we buy in Taiwan, providing you save me that and more." I said, "Okay."

We flew to Taiwan and went to his umbrella vendor. He was buying 75,000 umbrellas, and he was paying $10 apiece. The owner was named Mark Ma. I looked at Mark and said, "You're not going to get his order this year. Your prices are too high. We need to get it for $6." He said, "Oh, that's impossible." I said, "Okay. That's the price he's going to pay. Take it or leave it. We're going to go down the street to Betsy Umbrella if you're not willing to do business." He said, "Wait a minute," and went into the office. I guess he talked to his wife and his father. He came back out with actual tears in his eyes and said, "We can't do $6. Would you take $7.75?" I said, "I'll tell you what. I'll take $7.50, and we'll call it a day." I saved Ray $2.50 on 75,000 umbrellas, and that was the start of the trip. We imported $8 million in that one trip, and I got 10% of $8 million.

BILL FORSTER, IS AN ENTREPRENEUR WITH 50 YEARS EXPERIENCE STARTING, GROWING AND SELLING COMPANIES.

He has done business in dozens of countries, and was a trailblazer in developing business in countries like Russia and South Africa.

Bill has devoted his life to helping others. He established the Forster Foundation, which has supported charitable organizations in the U.S. and Israel.

Bill's autobiography, *If it Hadn't Been for my Wife, I'd be Living in a Trailer*, is available on Amazon.

TO CONTACT BILL

✉ bill@forsterholdings.com

🔗 https://www.forsterholdings.com/

CHAPTER 12

GROWING & SELLING A BUSINESS

Jeff Hollander

Julian: To start, can you tell us a bit about yourself and your business career?

Jeff: I'm originally from New Jersey. I started working at a family company called Hollander Home Fashions making bed pillows, mattress pads, and down comforters. I spent 30 years there running the company and selling it to a private-equity firm. I added another five years with them before I started getting into private equity myself, which ultimately led me into my newest company, Medigap Life, which is a Medicare insurance agency based in North Carolina, New York, and South Florida. Hollander Sleep Products, which is what Hollander Home Fashions is now called, provided about 50% of the bed pillows, mattress pads, and down comforters in the United States. Most of you are probably sleeping with me or else you know somebody who's sleeping with me. That company was started by my grandfather and father in 1953. I joined in 1979 and helped grow it from an $8 million company to a $400 million company when I sold it to Huntsman Gay Private Equity.

Julian: That's an amazing success story, but you started other businesses right after you had this very large one. Maybe you can tell us how you got into scaling a new business and some of the things that worked for you when you had to start from the ground up.

Jeff: I first started getting involved with a dozen companies through a private-equity firm and just dabbled in them but not really feeling I could have a big impact. I then joined one of my other partners, Jay Schwartz, and we decided we would create our own companies or buy small companies that we could scale, and that has been most successful for me. The one that I've been doing now is Medigap Life. We sell Medicare policies for Humana, Mutual of Omaha, Anthem, WellCare, and a number of other well-respected insurance carriers, and we grew the company from five agents to 150 agents in four years with some great partners. We actually were just acquired a few months ago by Alliant Insurance, which is a multi-billion insurance company out of California.

Julian: Another very impressive success. What piece of advice can you give to new business owners who want to become you?

Jeff:

The first thing to recognize is you've got to have trusted partners. You've got to understand all aspects of your business, and you've got to let your employees and your partners know what the entire business is about. The more people feel that they're part of the team, the more they're going to be empowered.

You also have to look at the long-term effects of your actions. You don't want to just solve a little problem today, not recognizing what the effects may be in the long term. Finally, staying with the same theme, you need to always value your employees. You need to be consistent and fair. You need to be honest always because your employees know when you're not, and if you're not honest with them, they're not going to be honest with you.

Julian: That's some very good advice. Now tell us about the selling. How do you start prepping for a sale? Is there a good time? Is there a bad time? Maybe you can walk us through that process, because I'm sure everyone who starts a business is always looking to see how they're going to cash out one day.

Jeff:

I think the time to start looking for a sale is when you see major changes happening in your company or your industry, and you don't feel that it's the right time for you to undertake them by yourself.

One example would be if you lost your passion for the business, because if you're not passionate about your business, your employees won't be passionate, and you're doomed. That's a time to look to make a change. Another time is when you see the industry making a major change, whether it's through consolidations or new legislation or new products out there in the marketplace. Those are times where it makes sense to be ahead of the curve and either consolidate with other companies in a joint sale or just sell yourself so that somebody else can grow it in the changing times.

Julian: When I sold my business back in '94, I did it for exactly some of the reasons you said. I used to sell to home centers, and when I entered the business, there were 500 home centers. When I exited the business, there were basically three: Home Depot, Lowe's, and Menards. I realized I would have to be with a conglomerate, or I was not going to be successful. You have to have the strength to be able to negotiate with these large retailers.

Jeff: It's very true, and sometimes you don't have a choice, but you need to recognize it before it's too late.

> I believe a business owner has a responsibility to keep the business open, to keep the employees employed, and to make sure their clients are getting the right product. That's a big responsibility. If you can't meet that responsibility, it makes sense to find another company that can come in and meet that responsibility to the employees and to the clients.

Julian: In my case, I sold within seven years, and I sold to a Fortune 500 company. My division went out of business, so they obviously were not a good steward of the company. What happened to Hollander after you sold?

Jeff: It has actually been sold three times, and it's larger than it was when I started with them, currently over a billion dollars in revenue. They've opened up new locations throughout North America, and they merged with another decor company because they felt the Hollander management was the stronger management for their portfolio companies. They've done well and we still have thousands of employees working here.

Julian: That's wonderful. I wish I could say the same. In your experience, when people sell their businesses, do they transition right into retirement, or do they go into another business?

Jeff: I think it depends on the individual. Generally, you're going to be assisting with the transition for six months, possibly up to five years, which is what I did because I had partners, Huntsman Gay, who I really liked and respected. I felt they recognized that people were more important than product and profits, and that's ultimately how you're going to have the greatest profits and the best company. I stayed five years, but I think that any business owner should try to stay with the company to get a smooth transition. Take your ego out of it and know that there are new owners who are going to run it the way they want to run it, but you want to be there to make sure your employees and your clients are able to get the continued good service you've been giving them for years.

The other thing I found is you need to find other businesses to be involved with. You can consult with other business owners to find your next passion, which is one of the things I did. I met with local business owners and gave them free advice about what I saw in industry in general, but I also found a lot of people who were very talented, some of whom I've been able to work with since then. That was nice. I've sat on a lot of nonprofit boards in the religious, education, housing, and medical fields, and I've been able to leverage my time and contacts into good ideas for the businesses we're working on that are nonprofits.

> The biggest fear I have for somebody who's leaving a business is this: If you don't have enough to do when you retire, you're going to be bored. You're used to running an enterprise; you're used to having 60-hour work weeks. You need to have a lot of hobbies. You need to have a lot of things to do, otherwise it will get boring. I would say don't sell unless you know what you're going to do next, because your activities are where happiness and enjoyment come from.

Julian: I couldn't agree with you more. In fact, as a financial advisor, I get a lot of people that say to me, "I can't wait to retire." I try to explain to them that retirement's not all it's cracked up to be. It's fun in the beginning, but you get bored very quickly if you retire too young. What advice would you give people when they sell as far as how they should manage their investments? What should they do first with all that money?

Jeff: Unless their business was in financial management, they need to have a wealth manager. They need to have somebody who's going to look at their holistic finances and lifestyle and recognize that they need a partner who specializes in financial management. In my case, I have Goldman Sachs. They don't manage all my money, but they oversee all my investments. They oversee what I do on my own, and I've made sure I'm giving them about 80% of my liquid assets to manage; I manage the other 20%, and I'm a little bit more risk taking than they are. They're protecting me from my own mistakes.

Julian: What is a large financial hurdle a business owner may have to overcome in building a business? I know we're going backwards because we've already sold the business, but just take a step back.

Jeff: Any time you're trying to grow a business, cashflow is always a challenge. You plan on your growth being able to finance itself, but that's not the reality in most industries. You've got to look for creative ways to bring in cash. You need to partner with your employees for cost savings, ideas, and productivity boosters, and you need to be honest and upfront with your lenders so they will be your partners and help you because they recognize that growth helps both sides.

Julian: What is your biggest challenge today?

Jeff: My biggest personal challenge is I'm looking for a new business to invest in with my partners. We've got a couple we're looking at in lead generation and in sports gaming, but we want to find the right business that we can scale and is meaningful for where the economy's going. However, the challenge with trying to get into any of those industries is creating environments that are conducive to today's workers. You've got to recognize that each individual has different needs, and you need to set a table for them to be good and productive at.

Over the last five years, I've seen less scrupulous competition in some industries, and you've got to deal with that. It's tough, because I still maintain you always have to be honest with yourself, your employees, and your clients. Dealing with bad competition is kind of difficult and something you've just got to stay above.

Julian: How would you define success?

Jeff: It's easy to look at a balance sheet and define success, and financial success is part of it: the ability to create stability for your organization, your family, and your network.

> But real success is knowing how you contributed to others. What did you give back to society, to your community, your friends, your family, and your employees that helps them have better lives?

So often people have come up to me and told me something I told them 10, 20 years ago, just little bits of advice that I gave because I care about people. That's my biggest success.

I'd like to share two things I found invaluable in my career. One is a quote from Yogi Berra: "You can observe a lot just by watching." Too often I would go to my various locations around the country, and I'd find my executives just telling the employees what to do. Nobody learned anything. But if we watched what they were doing, we learned and they learned. We collaborated and we partnered.

Lastly, Mike Ditka said, "Success isn't permanent and failure isn't fatal." Try to show a consistent front to your employees and your clients. Let them know everything is under control. When things look like they're at their worst, make it fun and enjoyable, and you'll get out of that pit and back to the success you're used to.

JEFF HOLLANDER SPENT THE BULK OF HIS CAREER AT HOLLANDER SLEEP PRODUCTS, A PRIVATELY HELD MANUFACTURER OF HOUSEHOLD TEXTILE PRODUCTS MARKETING TO ALL LEVELS OF DISTRIBUTIION.

There he won numerous industry awards on the way to becoming the largest US supplier of bed pillows, mattress pads and down comforters. Jeff is currently a Private Investor, with significant involvement managing Medigap Life, a multi-State insurance agency specializing in Medicare products that is differentiated though our proprietary software platforms.

Jeff has been very active in the community and has served on many non-profit boards including homeowner's associations, education, food insecurity, and healthcare.

TO CONTACT JEFF

✉ jh@jeffhollander.com

🔗 https://www.medigaplife.com/

CHAPTER 13

PROTECTING YOUR BUSINESS

Jared Stark

Julian: You've had an interesting career. It's not the standard law you're practicing now. Why don't you tell us a bit about your career and what you're doing now?

Jared: When I graduated law school, I worked at a huge firm in Washington, D.C. Then I came back down to Florida where my family is, and was in-house counsel for a little bit. I've always been entrepreneurial, so I ended up forming my own firm, went solo, and I've been doing that ever since. I recently also started another project, Stark & Company, which sells legal forms and templates. It's basically the easiest way to get contracts without having to go through the whole process of hiring a lawyer and waiting for the turnaround time. At this point, I've basically done the big-firm thing, the in-house thing, the small-firm thing, and the entrepreneurial thing. I have done every aspect of law, pretty much, except government.

Julian: Is it just business law, or do you also do personal-law documents?

Jared: Right now, it's really just business-law documents. That's where I focused my career over the last decade or so. I work primarily with startups, entrepreneurs, and small-to-medium-sized businesses.

Julian: I assume I would be like employment agreements or non-competes, things of that nature?

Jared: Exactly. At this point, I've done every document under the sun that a business could need. But I'd say the most common ones are employment agreements or offer letters for employees, independent-contractor agreements, master-service agreements for service providers, vendor agreements, non-disclosure agreements, all that fun stuff.

There are two sides to my business. I've got the practice itself where people can come if they need actual legal services. The other side is the forms and templates. We do have customer service through email. If people have questions or need some general guidance as to which form they need, we provide that as well.

Julian: What drew you to this type of law?

Jared: I've always been entrepreneurial. When most people go to law school, the goal is to work for the biggest firm they can find or to go into government and maybe become a prosecutor or public defender. I always had the goal of starting my own firm. I always knew that's where I'd be eventually. I've just always been entrepreneurial, and I saw law as a good way to get there. I was attracted to the idea of helping other people start and grow their businesses. That's what drew me to it, and it's been rewarding being able to help people do that.

Julian: On the client side of your practice, what is something you share with each client? Is there one major piece of advice you give to every client?

Jared: Every client is different, and they're in different stages of growth with their businesses.

> But one thing that's true for everyone, no matter where you are, is before you really get started with anything, you should do a trademark search.

A lot of people don't think about that. They know they've got to form their company, whether it's an LLC or a corporation. Maybe they've heard they should talk to an accountant about an S-Corp election. That's all great. But the first thing you should do if you've got a name in mind and you plan on using it is a federal trademark search to make sure nobody else is using a similar name.

If you don't, you could have clients, and you could be absolutely crushing it on the business side, but a year down the road, someone else using the name can sue you for infringement and basically make you rebrand your entire company, which can be a disaster. Make sure you do a trademark search or contact an attorney to do a trademark search before you start using it.

Julian: It's interesting you say that. For my very first business, we did a name search, and about two years later, we got sued anyway. It was not a problem because it was a frivolous case, but it was a good thing that we did a search, because we were going to use that name. We switched it, and it turned out not to be a problem.

Jared: I'm glad it worked out. But yes, even when you do your homework, and you use a name you think looks secure, trademark law is such a gray area. There's so much subjectivity to it that you could still have someone come out of the woodwork and file some frivolous lawsuit against you anyway, and that's just the nature of it.

Julian: I think in my case, it was just a scare tactic. Once we responded correctly, they just went away. It wasn't a big deal.

Jared: Often it is a scare tactic. I sometimes see larger companies that can use their war chests to sort of beat their competitors into submission. Your name might not even be that similar to theirs, but they send a cease-and-desist letter anyway to try and scare you off even when it's a very weak case. I see that all the time.

Julian: What is your unique approach that separates you apart from the competition?

Jared: There are a couple ways. First, we typically work on a flat-fee basis. It's attractive to a lot of small businesses or startups because you can contain your pricing and budget accordingly. Hourly pricing can get a little crazy and can become runaway when you have no idea what the bill's going to be at any given month. Being flexible on flat-fee pricing has helped us to become a bit easier to work with for true startups.

Another thing that sets us apart is that since we're a small firm, it's very one-on-one. You're not going to be speaking to a legal assistant or a paralegal, and you're speaking to someone who is a business owner.

> A lot of lawyers have a very lawyerly mindset. They're not thinking about getting the deal done. They're thinking about how to over-engineer it. In the back of my mind, I'm always thinking about how do we get this done? How do we get this done properly? How do you get to the finish line? I'm a business person and I understand that. I think that's a big deal.

Julian: I know you worked at Latham. Did they ever do flat billing, or are the big firms all hourly?

Jared: I did start my career at Latham. Hourly billing is the most prominent model. It's possible they had some alternative fee arrangements, but at that point in my career, those decisions were definitely above my pay grade.

Julian: What was it like there, at the second largest firm in the country?

Jared: Latham's a great firm. It was a great place to start a career. I was only there for about a year or so, and then I came back down to Florida, but my experience there was great. You work with some of the smartest lawyers you'll ever meet. You work on extremely complex matters and cases with huge values behind them, and you get the best training. The people you work with have created such great infrastructure and systems and training. I'm not trying to do an ad here for Latham, but it was a good experience, and it's a good place to start a career, or any big firm for that matter. If you are a lawyer and you've got options, starting at a large firm is helpful in a lot of ways in terms of building the right skillset and also the right approach to work.

Julian: You're getting a foundation that works, otherwise they wouldn't be who they are. My kids went to a private school, and they say the biggest thing they got out of that was learning how to study and prepare for a test. Very few people have the opportunity to work at a Top-100 law firm.

Jared: It can be tough to get in, but I think it's a good place to start, for sure.

Julian: You're obviously still young and getting started, but how do you define success?

Jared: I don't feel young anymore. I'm in my mid-30s, and I have young kids and a busy household. I guess my definition of success is changing. It's evolving. At this point, it's actually about working a little bit less and finding time to make sure you are available to create memories with your kids and be a good parent. When I was in my 20s, and I was first going out as a solo attorney, I would work late into the night. I would do whatever it took to grow the firm. At this point, I'm still working hard, still meeting people and promoting the firm and doing a good job for my clients, and I'm happy to do that. But I'm trying to focus more on making sure that I can be there to enjoy my kids.

The world has changed so much recently. There are more hybrid work opportunities than ever. I have an office, but I work from home most days, and I'm here to have dinner with my kids every night. We have dinner together, and we have breakfast together. Usually, they're banging on the door of my home office at 3:00 PM when they get home from school, and we hang out for a little bit, and then we have dinner. Being able to take advantage of that is the way I measure success now.

Julian: What do you wish you knew when you started that you know now? What's one thing you wish you could have known getting into law?

Jared:

> That burnout is real. You can burn out very easily. I've been there, and you have to be able to know when to say no to a client, when to set limits on yourself, and how to grow in a sustainable way.

In some ways it's generic advice, but you've got to be careful about how you grow your business or how you grow your professional career to make sure that you're building it sustainably.

Julian: What would you say is your biggest challenge right now?

Jared: The biggest challenge is finding that work-life balance. I think that's true for a lot of people—making sure you're happy and busy professionally and you're still finding the work to be a challenge, but in a good way, while also having the time to enjoy all the reasons you're working. That's always a challenge. I think it's a little bit of a give-and-take here and there. Right now, I'm in a good place as far as that goes, but it's always a balance.

Julian: What would you say is your biggest business challenge?

Jared: Scaling is difficult. I've been fortunate to work with great clients over the years, and I'm always meeting great new clients, but scaling is difficult for any business, and it's difficult in a law firm because you're selling your time and people want to speak to you. I like to develop those relationships with clients. But conversely, that makes it very difficult to scale, because you don't want to just put all your work on somebody else, and it's hard to maintain that relationship. Ultimately, I want to keep growing while maintaining my personal touch, and that has been challenging for me.

JARED STARK IS THE FOUNDER AND MANAGING ATTORNEY OF THE STARK BUSINESS LAW PLLC.

 Jared graduated from law school at Georgetown University and began his career at Latham & Watkins LLP, one of the largest and most prestigious corporate law firms in the United States. He then worked as in-house counsel for a large real estate development company before leaving to launch his own firm focused on providing corporate legal guidance to entrepreneurs, startups, and established companies.

In addition to corporate matters, Jared also maintains an active **trademark practice and has registered more than 500 trademarks for clients.**

Jared has been featured in the Miami Herald, the Daily Business Review, and other publications.

TO CONTACT JARED

✉ jstark@starkbusinesslaw.com
🔗 https://starkbusinesslaw.com/

NOW WHAT?

T hank you for reading this book. I trust you found the interviews to be as informative as I did. I hope this book showed you the importance of proper financial planning. My goal was to empower you to make financial decisions, even if you still need to take that first step. I want everybody to be able to successfully manage their money and feel confident in their financial future.

My intent was to give you the information necessary to make smart choices with your money. I want you to find the right path that will lead you to financial freedom. So let me ask the question at the top of this page.

Now what? What will you do with the information you received?

The important thing is that you do something. The biggest mistake people make is to not do anything. Not make decisions. Not make plans.

Chances are, there were times while reading this book you said, "I didn't realize that." If so, I hope your next thought was, "I can do something about that."

So, if nothing else, I hope this book will inspire you to take action. Take a look at the big picture. And not just your financial picture. Your life. Your goals. What do you want your retirement to look like?

You can also utilize the experts and other professionals in this book as a resource. They not only shared their knowledge with you, they also shared their contact information at the end of their chapter. They're happy to answer any follow-up questions you may have.

There's one other important step you can take. Because you have this book, you're entitled to a complimentary "Financial Freedom" consultation with me. That's a strategy session where we can get to know each other and I can answer all your questions. I may even answer ones you didn't think to ask!

If you'd like to get it scheduled, my contact information is on the next page.

Taking control of your financial life can be challenging. But with the right information, you can overcome those obstacles and meet your goals.

American Asset Management, Inc.

Schedule a
FINANCIAL FREEDOM
CONSULTATION

CONTACT: **Julian Rubinstein**

✉ julian@americanasset.com   📞 561-654-6010

YOUR GOAL IS **FINANCIAL FREEDOM.**
OUR GOAL IS **TO MAKE IT HAPPEN.**
www.americanasset.com

WANT TO
PUBLISH A BOOK
LIKE THIS?

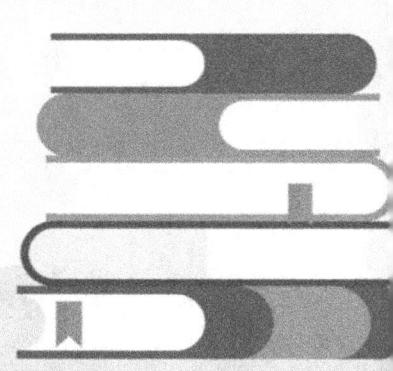

BMD PUBLISHING HAS PUBLISHED DOZENS OF BOOKS LIKE THIS IN NUMEROUS BUSINESS SECTORS.

OUR PROCESS IS EFFICIENT AND EFFECTIVE.

IF YOU'VE ALWAYS WANTED TO DO A BOOK BUT DIDN'T KNOW WHERE TO BEGIN, GO TO WWW.MARKETDOMINATIONLLC.COM/BMDPUBLISHING TO SET UP A FREE *TURN THE PAGE* CONSULTATION.

BEGIN AN EXCITING NEW CHAPTER IN YOUR LIFE!

IT'S YOUR TIME TO BECOME
AN AUTHOR

www.ingramcontent.com/pod-product-compliance
Lightning Source LLC
Chambersburg PA
CBHW071044290526
45795CB00004B/1303